THIS THING CALLED REAL-ATIONSHIPS

Build to last ... Work to enjoy

Maria L Harbajan

THE PUBLISHER'S
NOTEBOOK LIMITED
"ENVISION IT, WE'LL PUBLISH IT"

2019

This Thing Called Real-ationships - Build to Last…Work to Enjoy

ISBN: 978-976-96192-9-6

ISSN: 0799-608X

Cover Art by: Dale Sewell – Geek Resources

Published by: The Publisher's Notebook Ltd

                   Email: publisher@thepublishersnotebook.com

THE PUBLISHER'S
NOTEBOOK LIMITED
"ENVISION IT, WE'LL PUBLISH IT"

DEDICATION

I affectionately dedicate this book to every person from childhood until now, who has helped me to become the woman that I am today. First of all, to my mother, Monica Stewart, 97 years old, who worked hard to raise three boys and a girl (me) with the help of a devoted sister, Beatrice and a big brother, Daniel who "fathered" me. I also dedicate this book to my sister from another mother, friend, and accountability partner from High School until now, Sharon Nash. Not sure where my life would be without your counsel, comfort, support and loving correction.

To every school, college and Sunday School teacher, who took special interest in my welfare. I make special mention of the late Rosemarie Vernon (Primary School teacher), Sister Patricia Schnapp (High School). Dr. Claire Henry, friend and lecturer in Seminary.

To Jackie (Morgan) Lucas who led me to the Lord at 15 years old and all those who along with her, discipled me, including Bishop Dr. Peter Morgan and Lt Col Raphael & Cherry Mason who played a critical role in being my spiritual parents.

To every true FRIEND – many and special deep friendships that I was blessed to have through the years. Special dedication to

Dawn Bennett who mentored me in Drama and allowed me to be in her home with her family at troubled transitional times of my young adulthood, dealing with my mixed-up moods and attitudes. Those friends who stuck closer than a brother in times when I truly needed you. Too many to list here.

Our son, Qowayne, gone too soon, but is a rose in God's heavenly garden now. Still missing you. To our affectionate son, our precious gift from God. There is nobody like you, DeMario. Our adopted adult daughter, Jenene who although coming recently into our lives and home, has brought joy. Then there are all our other children, spiritual and otherwise, whose presence in my life has increased and fulfilled my desires to be a special kind of mother.

Last but certainly not least – my precious husband, Devon, who next to Jesus, is the best male I have ever encountered, having such a balance of godliness and gentle firmness; an ability to push me into my God-given destiny without being threatened by my progress or status; an ability to assist, even in menial activities to ensure that I fulfill my God-given roles. A rare gem of a man. My gift from God. The one with whom I can have real-ationship.

Thanks to all of you for giving to the Lord. My life has been a fulfilled one, because you have loved me and have allowed me to love you. You have in many ways taught and allowed me to be REAL in my relationships.

CONTENTS

FOREWORD

By Counselling Psychologist- André Allen-Casey

I have recently coined a phrase, "give me the Facts, not your Faith, Feelings or Fictions." I have received many push backs in my deliberations of this phrase considering feelings are sought after for validation and vindication. This book has provided me with the unequivocal Facts, reinforced my Faith, informed my Feelings and absolutely gave no Fiction. The writer's own experiences in her Real-ationships' journey has more than qualified her as an authority in relationships.

From the womb to the tomb we have experienced the importance of "not becoming bitter but better" irrespective of our interpretation of our situation. We have learnt the value of spending quality TIME with our children providing a foundation for them to make the correct choices and to understand their Male/Female differences especially during the various stages of their development. We gained meaningful insights on the right and wrong reasons for getting married, to remarry and how to manage deal breakers. We also embarked upon a journey which spoke about the role, the goal and even the myths and solutions of sexual interactions.

This book on Real-ationships further exposed us to the need of adoption, the impact of fasting, the worth of friends and the cautions of dealing with the enemy. As this exhilarating book slowly comes to a close, we are reminded of the hills and valleys, the pain and hurt along with the triumphant victories that families will encounter.

Finally, this enthralling and nothing short of an inspirational book, closes its chapters with the amazing life journey and conversion of its author (Maria L Harbajan). I sincerely hope that as you make your expedition through this book you will (as I have) discover the unequivocal Facts, your Faith reinforced, your Feelings re-informed and you would have not been misinformed. This is truly a bestseller and a must read for all the sexes but especially to our mothers and daughters who may have not started well but will learn how to finish better and not bitter.

Andre' Allen-Casey has been a Christian for over 30 years, a Counselling Psychologist for over 8 years, and is currently a Professional Therapist at Family Life Ministries in Jamaica.

PREFACE

What many people might not know about me is that I am nourished by relationships. Not in a codependent manner, although in the past I did. I find much of my fulfillment in life in building, maintaining and giving of myself in various types of relationships. I am very relational and have a passion for seeing relationships work! This, I believe is the reason I chose to become a professional counsellor and Minister of Religion and why I chose to write on Relationships as my third book. The title is Real-ationships, because in my journey and seasons in every type of relationship, there is a key I have found – BE REAL!

I don't know of anything else that can so enrich one's life or devastate one's psyche than dealing with close blood or non-blood relationships. Much of the damage in relationships comes however, because we are not real with each other. We wear masks. Sometimes, the ugly ones of selfishness and self-preservation, that damage the relationships that we interminably need or simply will have in our lives.

I waited with excitement to do this book but realized one day in prayer, that it might be a troublesome task, as to do service to this undertaking, one will have to go deeper than was anticipated, expose more of oneself than is desirable and may even have to awaken old painful memories that were long buried and forgotten. But when I consider how other people's painful experiences had helped me as they shared and made themselves vulnerable or by caring, I thought, it is worth the risk!

Many did not discover that there are risks involved in all types of relationships until they ventured into the deep and gave their hearts to someone, whether that someone was a child, friend or lover. Relationships is one of those things that can bring a smile to one's face when a day is not going right; a change in one's mood at the sight of a loved one, whether in the form of a flashing memory or they are there, in your eyesight. It can conjure up a pain in one's heart, or a strong desire to live or to die. It amazes me to hear medical professionals declare that many seriously ill persons may choose to or not to walk out of a hospital based on a will to or not to live and this is oftentimes tied to **relationships** in their lives or the lack of it.

Relationships impact us in every way and the following chapters will explain how and what to do when the experience is a painful one, who to turn to in time of need and some valuable lessons that this author has learnt through bruises, scratches and brokenness coming through the seasons of life. It would be my joy to know that you will benefit from my experiences as I have from others. I hope that you will embrace the mountain top experiences and the valleys that come even within great friendships, marriages, business and family relationships. It is my intention to help you to find that ultimate fulfilling relationship which I found since I was fifteen years old – a relationship with the ultimate Father, Friend, Lover and Partner. His Name is Jesus.

As you go through this book, my hope is that you will embrace God's gift to mankind – relationships and that you will be encouraged to walk through and find healing for difficult ones. I pray that you will find the strength in God to change toxic relationships and you will celebrate that thing that has brought the greatest joys into our lives even though mixed with pain – it is this thing called Real-ationships.

I am asking my readers to proceed with open hearts and a clear understanding that nothing written in this book, even when the naked truth has to be exposed, is written from a heart of malice or with any intention of causing more pain instead of healing. Remember that the human experience is common to man, so if any incident resembles your own, whether you are known to me or not, you are among a crowd of participants on this platform of life. Being so captivated by the dynamics of relationships, I do read a lot and have watched many movies dealing with different accounts of persons' lives and experiences. That is one of my pastimes. From life's entire grand movie, I have gleaned and written, hoping to help you succeed and overcome.

ACKNOWLEDGEMENTS

I wish to express my deepest appreciation to God who allowed me the opportunity to write this book using my pain to be someone else's gain; my test to be someone else's rest; my struggles and victory to be someone else's key to rising up out of their "ashes".

To all the persons in my life who have challenged me to be real, including my various teachers and lecturers.

To Sylvia Dallas and her team who as usual, played the part of being more than publishers, gave invaluable advice and generally went beyond the call of duty to help me produce this book.

To all those who contributed, allowing themselves to be vulnerable so that my readers would see a real-ationship in action.

To Andre Allen-Casey who so graciously wrote the foreword. As a senior coach in the area of counselling psychology, he is helping many through his individual counselling, family therapy, seminars and guest appearance on radio programmes, to enjoy their real-ationships.

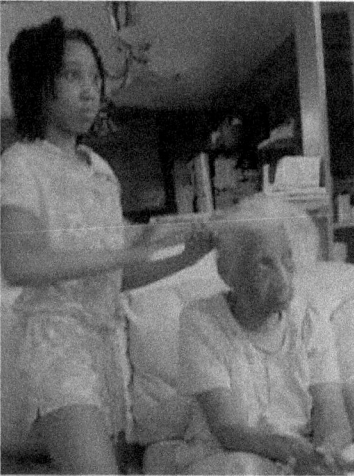

An amazing connection though four generations apart

INTRODUCTION

From the Womb to the Tomb

The journey between what you once were and who you are now becoming is where the dance of life really takes place

–Barbara de Angelis

One of the most exciting news that a man and woman can have is, "You are going to have a baby!" This is a source of great joy, as long as the couple is open to welcoming a new life. The value, dignity and passion for life come alive as each considers that they are about to produce after their own kind, and for those who opt for fostering and adoption, it's still the excitement that "I have a young life into whom I can pour myself". The next months are caught up with planning and executing the plan to allow this young life to invade their space and their hearts. When it is a biological child, a relationship starts even within the womb, as the mother relates to the child that is signaling by kicks that he/she will be coming soon.

The father who is able by touch, feel this movement, begins to feel the excitement and/or dread of added responsibility coming to his life. The children who are allowed to participate in this adventure, share in this anticipation, wondering what this new life will be like. Each family member could be pondering and experiencing mixed feelings about what the entrance of this new life could bring.

From the beginning of life within the womb, we begin to form a chain of relationships. Studies have shown that the unborn child recognizes voices within his/her environment, particularly, those that speak directly to that unborn child. Though persons are not seeing this life with their physical eyes, they communicate with the one they know will eventually burst forth into a brand new world. When this child enters the world, everything changes – even relationships! For children, it is no longer mother and father but one more person in their space. For the parents, it is a change of schedule; one more person to provide for; one more person to take to the doctor. One more set of teachers with whom one will need to interact as this child moves through school. One more life to train up in the way he/she ought to go, trusting God that he/she will not depart from it. It becomes a journey and an adventure that will have its bumps and at times, a roller-coaster ride especially through the teenage years as this child and the family work on building relationships. Both the child and parents have to constantly be working through the perimeters of their relationship, as the child and the parents go through different developmental stages. This we will deal with in depth in the next chapter on parent-child relationships.

As this child goes through life, he/she has to learn to relate to siblings, other relatives within and outside of the home. He/She has to learn how to get along with neighbours, adults and children within the school environment and also within their place of worship. They even develop casual relationships along the way, with those who transport them and serve them within the sphere of the marketplace. The child's educational life and social interactions will see the formation of different sets of relationships, moving from one educational institution to another, one neighbourhood to another and changing places of worship. These relationships will not be static but will have varying degrees of dynamism and some will be formed out of strong interests and passions that will either serve to make or break the human psyche.

After meandering through the years of a succession of events and various relationships, made and broken, soon the parents are being introduced to another relationship that can change all of their lives – a potential spouse! To this spouse they will have to adjust themselves; checking their own standards and prejudices, wondering if they or their offspring is ready for such a step in life. Introduced in their lives, is another set of relationships, the potential spouse's family. Things are great if they have a special liking or love for their offspring's new attachment(s). But what if this is not the case? How do they deal with any hint of

x

disagreement with their child's choice which could negatively affect even the most solid parent-child relationship? They are called upon to carefully and wisely meander their way through their own thoughts and emotions surrounding this choice that they cannot make for their treasured child. The following chapter will look in more depth at this dilemma.

A union develops and if they are in agreement they can welcome a "daughter" or "son" into their family, at this later stage of their and their child's life. Hopefully it is one that they are proud to have their photo displayed in their home or at work. But what if they are not at peace about his/her selection? Now they are "compelled" to attend a wedding, invite a not favourite daughter or son-in-law to special family functions; deal with grand-children that may exhibit more of the genes of the "unwelcomed" in-law. They have to choose to relate to their child's choice of intimate relationship. This may be for the rest of their existence on earth.

It is amazing how each entrance of a different relationship in one individual's life can transform that person positively or negatively and can impact those around with whom he/she relates. There are no neutral relationships within the sphere of family, friendships or fraternities. Each person is being influenced. Each person is being impacted. Decisions are being made within each context that will change the course of one's existence in one way or another. Hopefully this influence is for good, because whether or not, a whole family, school, community, institution, organization and nation can be changed for a lifetime by one life and one type of relationship. Have you ever seen a life that is overtaken by drugs or crime and how all of the above-mentioned areas pay a price in one way or another? Can you see how persons who come into contact with this individual sometimes wish that either they or the individual was dead – not having to experience this painful journey in life?

Then there is the approaching the "winter of life" – getting older. The fears that sometimes come. Health issues; whether we will be dependent or independent; will be aging alone or with family and companionship? The experience of seeing close friends departing this life and the wondering of, when will my time come? The questions of competence; sharpness of various faculties and senses; moving into unfamiliar environments that might be necessary for security; the possible loss of dignity as the need for assistance increases.

Relationships impact us in every way from birth till death. The following chapters will explain how they do. The challenges that are common will be expressed and addressed with some possible solutions to these difficulties. The benefits and fulfillment of various types of relationships will be lauded.

THIS THING
CALLED
REAL-ATIONSHIPS

Build to last..Work to enjoy

A CHILD - An Unfathomable Gift from God to the Home

CHAPTER ONE

EARLY BEGINNINGS: PARENT-CHILD RELATIONSHIP

*"When you thought i wasn't looking, i
heard you say a prayer, and i
believed there is a god i could always
talk to. When you thought i wasn't
looking, i felt you kiss me goodnight,
and i felt loved. When you thought i
wasn't looking, i saw that you cared,
and i wanted to be everything that i
could be."*

mary rita schilke korazan

Where is the Manual? Which Manual? The one that shows us
how to be good parents! Yes, we all wish we had a 'How to Do It'
Manual for Parenting but there is not one such manual that fits all
parents for all children in all cultures. Parenting can be a lonely
journey, and this does not depend on whether it is a single-parent

family or not. The rigours of successfully taking children through each developmental stage, dealing with all the temperamental and personality hiccups, doing the balancing act of school life, social life, sports life, religious life, home life with them, especially when there are more than one, is overwhelming for many. Some parents have thrown in the towel, escaped in their jobs, hobbies, social activities, addictions or migration. Whatever the challenges, children are a blessing! The Bible does tell us that "children are a heritage from the Lord, The fruit of the womb is a reward (Psalm 127:3 – NKJV)

One command that God has given to the human race that He has also given us the pleasure to fulfill is to be fruitful, multiply and replenish the earth (Gen. 1:22). This was God's idea as He wanted us to produce after our kind. This command has at times been handled responsibly, recklessly, involuntarily and in some cases regrettably. Children have been produced in happy and also contentious environments; with fathers known and celebrated and fathers never known because of rape or some form of activity the "doped" mother was unconscious of. Therefore, the children who the Scriptures tell us are "an heritage of the Lord" are either experienced as a gift or "something" that we are carrying that is a curse! While some couples languish with the desire to produce their own offspring, others who have been fruitful sometimes curse the day that they conceived! The latter scenario is usually based on relationships and the type of atmosphere and circumstances under which a child is conceived. Usually if the child-bearing was planned for and desired by both parents, the results are different.

I recall once being asked to intervene in a child-bearing crisis. This was while going through a "midnight experience" of my own – a relationship that almost wrecked my life, reputation and ministry! I intervened only because of my relationship with the person who sent the SOS. Some details I will leave out to protect the identity of the persons involved. The context was one of rape and resultant pregnancy. Apart from an unplanned and unwanted pregnancy that came through violation, the young lady was afraid of her parents discovering this, further damaging an already brittle relationship between herself and one of her parents. This fear is a strong one in my culture since many are warned not to ever disrupt their education and that they will be excommunicated from the home, if they should bring home a child produced especially while they are a teenager. This expectant student, though not a teen, was panicking. Her only solution was to kill the child she was carrying or to kill herself. Murder or suicide! I was forced to step aside from my own crisis and to help in this situation. After intervening with counselling and presenting possible alternatives, e.g. foster care and adoption, suggesting a place where the young lady could live until she had the child, praying and covering her in God's love, hope stepped into the picture. She embraced the options presented.

Closer to the time of her delivery, we decided to have a baby shower for her. We found out that her parents were now informed and instead of the horrible outcome that she anticipated, she was shown love and compassion. At the small and private shower, when asked what the decision was that was made as she was approaching her time of delivery, her response startled us. "I am not giving up **my** baby!" What a contrast to what I heard at the beginning! The fetus moved from a "thing" intruding within her womb and about to destroy her life and future, to "my baby". Wow! We, in one voice, gave God the praise and continued to discuss the process of delivery and aftercare. Although the circumstances were unfortunate and her body was violated, she began to form a bond with the child in her womb. That unexplainable attachment that begins to form between parent and child once they are aware that their own 'flesh and blood' is developing and will one day, come screaming into the world, is startling.

The Waiting Can Be Gruelling

Some couples, like us, had to go through the arduous tests, doctors' visits, painful examinations and several negative pregnancy results. This can go on for over a decade for many couples. The union is sometimes severely tested as each negative pregnancy-result, even if hid from the other, can cause deep pain and disappointment. There is a "dark hole" of depression into which some couples sink. The question of should I keep going through this – having to read these negative results; having to hear from the doctors that something did not work; asking the question over and over again, "What's wrong with me/us?" "Why are persons who don't want, are aborting babies or don't love children, able to have?" If you are a person of faith, it may be even more difficult to accept that God has not "opened your womb" and if so, why not? Some couples are damaged in the area of their self-esteem especially if they are in a context where having children of your own is a sign of manhood and for the woman not being a "mule"(a derogatory expression used in some cultures to mean, barren). Some religious, family and social contexts are avoided because of the constant questions and repetitious answers that often come up once the couple find themselves in those surroundings.

After waiting, the day may finally come when the result is positive. I am pregnant! The cloud of the "shame" of impotence in child-bearing is now lifted. The couple is excited to make the grand announcement. We are able! I can still remember that look on my husband's face when he saw the pregnancy test – positive! It's a smile that is indescribable. One full of all sorts of emotions and warming the heart of the observer. The preparations are on the way. Care is being taken not to disrupt the life of that delicate fetus. We worked hard and waited long. We cannot afford to make any blunders, was our resolve. For some that happy day comes, when for the first time they hear that baby cry. Tears, laughter, releasing of balloons, sending of video clips and photos of the few hours old baby. "She is here!" "He is here!" "They are here!"

But it can be the final curtain closing, as the scenario ends differently for others. It's the deep dark hole of disappointment, which we also experienced, of hearing, something has gone wrong and watching this child, leave your life, involuntarily, from the womb, not alive!

"Miscarriage affects about 25 percent of women who become pregnant during their lifetime." [https://www.aamft.org] Apart from miscarriages, there are stillbirths, occurring in about 1% of pregnancies, Sudden Infant Death Syndrome (SIDS) - the most frequent cause of death in children under one year of age. Whatever the reason, the results are the same. A broken heart, empty arms, empty cribs, painful memories, broken dreams and sometimes the dissolution of a marriage! Grief...grief...grief!

In my case, it was listening to the doctor's pronouncement followed by compassionate prayers offered by her. "If the bleeding stops then there is a chance that the baby will live but...". I remember silently praying as I walked back to my car, asking God for 3 things if it was inevitable and in His providential will, in spite of my strong faith: "Let it happen at home; let it happen when no visitor is there; and let my husband be nearby." Those prayers were answered. A visitor had just left the house and I went to the bathroom observing that the bleeding had not stopped. Suddenly I heard "plop, plop, plop" as the pieces of my "dream child" made from love, began to vanish from my/our lives. Yes, we were devastated. We lost the battle. Though this happened fourteen years ago, the memory of that day is still one that I don't readily want to recall. But it was just a fetus, one might exclaim. It was not yet born! Those who have felt this bond will identify with this pain. Those who know that from conception to birth, there is a life growing inside will understand. Those who like my husband had already begun to bond with the child, talking to him/her in the womb. Those who know that God already begins to write the book of a child's life like He did with the prophet Jeremiah (Jeremiah 1: 4, 5) will empathize.

Everything went quiet after that bathroom experience, except for the sound of my husband speaking with my doctor on the phone and hearing that he has to leave for a while to fill a prescription that the doctor was calling in to the nearby pharmacy. You would not believe the loss we felt! Those who have walked this road will identify and hopefully as you are reading, God's love and His Hand of healing will be upon you. In only a few months, we had become attached to this child. My husband spoke to the fetus. We prayed and were thankful every day. But it was not to be. Depression set in. We had tried for so long and I, in particular, had undergone even laparoscopic surgery in the process of examining and fixing the issue of infertility. Some of the tests, one in particular was extremely painful. I have vivid memories of the day at the lab. I wonder how I did not pass out on that table! When ovulation restarted, for the first time, I experienced vertigo. Driving to the hospital, everything in sight on the journey was spinning! Weird. After all of this, then getting pregnant, then losing the baby! It was devastating!

There was a baby, Qowayne, who we had brought into our home when he was five months old. We were asked to help when his mother faced some unfortunate circumstances in life. We had bonded with him in the year and couple of months that he was with us, and loved him like our own flesh and blood. Although we were grieving the loss of our biological baby, we were thankful for him and his presence brought much joy. One day as he stood at the front door, he looked up at me and said, "Mommy" and that was like divine touch upon my soul! When we were given an all-expense paid consolation vacation after our bereavement, we gladly took him along. He was too young to know and to understand but his talking and laughter in the vehicle and even the quiet breathing heard when he finally fell asleep was music to our ears. We realized that God, foreseeing that this would happen, brought him into our home and into our hearts. He became a son and moved into our home. His presence, and DeMario, our other son who came into our lives later, filled our lives and home with happiness.

Coping with the Loss of a Child Through Death

Only he who feels it knows! If there is a context where this is true, it is with the loss of a child! Parents/guardians expect their children/ward to bury them and not the other way around. Qowayne's tragic departure from this life, three months before his 4th birthday was another devastating event that we all had to walk through. While playing he fell into a manhole that was filled with water that was left uncovered by someone in the apartment complex in which we lived. He drowned before we could get him out. Now two children gone! More grief.

Whether the child was lost in the womb or sometime after existence in the world, the pain can be the same. It is the pain that comes to a parent/guardian who has truly bonded with a child. They had a real-ationship. This relationship goes much deeper than eyes can see. It has inbuilt within it, hope, dreams, expectations for the future, images of life's stages – pre-school, kindergarten, entering High School and maybe college, marriage, grand-children. This was already a photo album in the mind, filled with the various events that this child's life would cover. "Over 57,000 children under the age of 19 die every year in the United States." *(American Association for Marriage and Family Therapy)* Those of us who have experienced this loss are far from being alone. It doesn't make the loss easier to know this, but we are able to empathize with other families who may be currently struggling with it. This pain is real and as we build real-ationships with others, may we be sensitive to this delicate pain of infertility or child mortality and reach out with an understanding heart.

I had to make some decisions that would help me to press on out of my own pain. I am choosing to be real and share with you my story as well as my nuggets that helped me to overcome. Here are some **suggestions** for you out of my experiences that might help you through your grieving and loss:

A Decision Not to be Bitter: One emotion that a person must resist when there is loss of someone who is dear to them is bitterness. If the person's life was snuffed out by tragedy or trauma, the more the temptation might be there to harbour bitterness. It's the anger and resentment that one feels when something valuable is taken from them and they did not voluntarily give it up. It's that out-of-control feeling that this experience is yours, like it or not! Some have never come out of that state of bitterness and thus have lost out on life; have caused much suffering for others who are left behind and may be attempting to walk through the aftermath of the loss themselves. Some grieving persons have embraced a self-destructive lifestyle that one wonders, if the loved one was still alive, how he/she would feel seeing this destruction. Here is a quote from my first book, **ARISE...Intercessors Arise**! A Manual for the Birthing, Calling, Training and Restoration of Prayer Warriors, 2015:

> *Becoming Better Not Bitter. This is a recognition that every experience, barring none, that God allows in our*

lives is for our betterment, never for our ruination. Jeremiah 29:11 reminds us that God's plans and thoughts for you are "thoughts of peace, and not of evil, to give you an expected end."(KJV) This is a mind-set that sustains one in all manner of circumstances and heartaches. This is the attitude that will allow us to truly come out of the murky waters of despair and disappointment and when you pass through the rivers, they will not sweep over you. When you walk through the fire, you will not be burned; the flames will not set you ablaze (Isaiah 43:2).

Life Happens; Trust God: We wish we had more control over what happens to us, but we don't. Life happens around us and things affect us. Some bemoan the fact that good things happen for "bad people" and bad things happen to "good people". The reasons for this are puzzling but the one fact that must be held firmly within our minds is that, God is never unfair or unjust (Jeremiah 29:11). God is always a good God in spite of what we experience. There is no evil or wickedness in God. He made the world perfect and man chose to corrupt it. Since God did not make robots but humans with a free will, we are able to choose right from wrong actions and unfortunately, whichever actions we choose, impacts others negatively or positively. There are consequences.

Many grieving parents question whether life will hold any meaning for them and wonder how they will survive the pain of their loss. Parents describe the feeling as having a hole in their heart that will never heal, and may blame themselves and ask, "If only I had." Or they may be angry with their spouse, the physician, God, or the government.

[https://www.aamft.org/imis15/AAMFT/Content/Consumer_U pdates/ Grieving_the_Loss_of_A_Child.aspx]

There is a reason behind anything God allows to happen and we might not be aware of that reason. This is where trusting in God comes in. A trust walk is never easy but it should not begin with tragedy. It should be a daily walk that will help us if/when tragedy strikes. We can place our hands in the Hands that rule the world and know according to Jeremiah 29:11 that His plans for us are good and not evil and it is to give us a prosperous future. The human experience will always be touched by pain and heartache. If you are not going through a painful experience now, chances are that you have had at least one in the past and if you live long enough, you will be having one in the future. As I heard someone say recently, "That's life; it is what it is!"

Give Your Heart to Love Again. It is really hard to watch others leave the hospital cuddling their newborn when you leave with your arms empty. When you watch your lost child's friends playing, growing up, graduating, marrying, etc. and knowing that you will never have those joys. It's hard when you are asked. 'How many children do you have?' and you have to pause to answer. Do I count only the living or do I include the dead with an explanation. A somewhat uncomfortable position to be in. Some have to answer, "None". That word for them can be like a dagger each time the question is asked and answered unless they choose to view their circumstances differently.

The thought of loving other people's children is out-of-the-question for some, especially if being asked to foster or adopt. The idea of attempting to have another biological child seems fruitless until one deals with the "What if" questions. What if I lose another pregnancy? Do I want to go through this sorrow ever again? Do I want to open my heart again in the same way only to suffer heartbreak? Apart from the fears of trying again, some people try to cope by finding themselves in an even worse scenario - shutting oneself away emotionally from loved ones, especially children, who are dependent on you for emotional sustenance. It is not unusual for the child/children left behind to be wondering, by the extreme and extended reaction to the loss, if this parent would rather the dead child to have been them or am I not worth much to you to continue to celebrate my life! Parents have to be mindful at this time that they have others to live for and there are others who are also grieving and attempting in the best way they know how, to cope with the loss.

My husband and I struggled with the balance when Qowayne died. Our hearts hurt so badly that we felt we were just carrying out our duties to survive. We still had to live but how would our "survival mode" be affecting our younger son? He needed more than that and he was still very young. He too was missing the other "pea" that was in his pod. Life had to be kept as normal and consistent for him, even with his missing companion and playmate. I remember saying to myself. "We can bounce back over time, but I will not allow anything to wreck his foundational development, emotionally or otherwise. I got to work, focusing on helping him through rather than focusing on myself. He still needed us to be there for him emotionally.

Another aspect to be mindful of are children who were close to or had any remote connection to the child when the loss, especially tragic, took place. That "child-witness" could end up blaming himself for the death! Even parents too have to be careful of the "blame game", whether it is blaming themselves or blaming others. It is natural to want to hold someone somewhere accountable for the death of your beloved. However, when the smoke clears and you can be rational, which should be within weeks of the death, please be careful that you do not attribute culpability to the wrong persons and destroy others and relationships. While you have to face the reality of your emotions, it might be better to talk them out with a counsellor or pastor who can be objective and neutral, listening to the reality of your experience and not with someone who would be feeling offended or feeling judged by you. Marriages have been destroyed, homes broken up, children become suicidal because of this error, playing the "blame-game", when dealing with grief. Let's be real. Truly, how long can someone live and relate healthily in a context where they know that their parent, intimate partner, other relative is blaming them for the death of a loved one?

What If God Rescued Our Loved One? This is one aspect to the mystery of death of our loved ones that we don't often explore but the Scripture does give this as one possible explanation. Isaiah 57: 1-2 (NASB)

> *The righteous man perishes, and no man takes it to heart;*
> *And devout men are taken away, while no one understands.*
> *For the righteous man is taken away from evil,*
> *He enters into peace;*

Although death is oftentimes viewed as an unavoidable evil, it is presented at least in one place in Scriptures as God's way of delivering some from "evil" to get him to a place of "peace". The first time when this revelation hit me was as we were comforting a family whose daughter's fiancé was killed in a motor vehicle accident. We were without words as we sat to try to grapple with this tragedy. While alone, however, and in prayer, God led me to this Scripture. When I shared it with the family afterwards, they were very encouraged and to my surprise, it was one of the Scriptures read at the funeral service.

Persons without collaborating have shared with a family that God "rescued" their loved one who died young. One of the persons who shared was weeping over the tragic loss when God comforted her by expressing to her that he rescued him before he felt the impact of the tragedy! I, having experienced a tragic loss of a child, have sought to comfort with counsel and prayer other parents who have experienced similar tragedies. One mother who lost her 2 year-old who drowned in a water tank that was left uncovered, after going through an encounter similar to losing her mind, came to a place of peace as we shared together. "God knows best" she uttered. I was surprised at the look of peace that came over her face. She was able to move on with her life after the funeral and returned or called to let me know of the progress she was making, including being able to return to work soon after. By attempting to deal with my own tragedy in a healthy way, I was at a place to comfort her in her own pain. This is how God wants us to comfort others after we have *received comfort from Him*. (2Cor 1:3-4)

There Are Some Things Worse Than Death! I have heard mothers bemoan the birth of a child who turned out to be a menace to society. They have even uttered a wish for their death if that was the only way to stop them from doing harm to others. Their child's death would be the way of escape for others. That they would be rescued from that offspring and victims are able to walk freely. It is sad though to think that a parent could come to this point where they would wish death for their loved one and it is not out of a bitter heart but one of altruism.

I have also encountered those parents who were not wishing for death of their loved one but rather that this child was never born. Their regret had nothing to do with the child's behaviour but the impact of the other parent's conduct on that child Children have suffered because of a revengeful parent when, for example, there is the cessation of the relationship between the parents. The child is used as a pawn to hurt the other parent. This child is constantly in pain emotionally and sometimes abused physically as he/she desires and needs to relate to the non-residential parent. School work gets affected; health issues turn up; negative behavioural changes occur and the list goes on.

Dealing With Disappointments Appropriately. One of my main weaknesses was dealing with disappointments. I hated being disappointed! It used to affect my prayer life. I would go to pray, and the words would not come then I had to acknowledge: I am disappointed with God! Or I am disappointed with someone else / some circumstance that I felt God had control over but did not do what I expected Him to do. What helped me to overcome? It was looking in God's Word at how others overcame. One person who spoke to me was King David in the Bible. I was able to identify too with the following quote and by being honest with myself, that I needed to work on this, my real-ationship with God and others began to improve in this area.

"... a veil was lifted from my eyes. I started to see what my problem was. I was expecting this life to be what it is not, and

*was never meant to be: perfect. And being the idealist that I am, I was struggling with every cell in my body to make it so. It had to be perfect. And I would not stop until it was. I gave my blood, sweat, and tears to this endeavor: making the world into heaven. This meant expecting people around me to be perfect. ... But herein lay my fatal mistake. My mistake was not in having expectations; as humans, we should never lose hope. The problem was in *where* I was placing those expectations and that hope. At the end of the day, my hope and expectations were not being placed in God. My hope and expectations were in people, relationships, means. Ultimately, my hope was in this world rather than God.*

Rubina [http://thoughtfulandinspirational.blogspot.com/]

So I had to deal with any skewed thinking, wherever that was found. I had to confront any myths I had about life, work, relationship, God. Sometimes it was a predisposition to feel like a victim especially when I got evil in return for the good that I had done. This is life! It is what it is. We cannot control what happens around the corners of life. We walk one day at a time; taking one step at a time and trusting the God Who knows and controls all things. Learning to trust took a weight off my shoulders, especially when dealing with disappointments.

Loss Through Crime and Violence

In Jamaica, a July 17, 2011 report stated that, "The number of child/teen killings between 2001 and 2010 could have easily doubled, as statistics published by the Planning Institute of Jamaica (PIOJ) show that 1,600 more were gunshot victims." [http://bit.ly/o3Rc48] What a horrible way to lose a child. To know that someone's selfish or wicked behaviour extinguished a life that they are unable to bring back to you. That's a different level of pain because now the parents have a perpetrator to deal with. There is a monument in Kingston, Jamaica, called the Secret Gardens. There posted are the names of the 664 children who died as a result of crime and violence.

> *Less than eight years after it was established, the Secret Gardens Monument in downtown Kingston is running out of space to record the names of Jamaica's children killed under violent and tragic circumstances.*
>
> *The Kingston and St Andrew Corporation (KSAC) last week added another 214 names to the monument located at the intersection of Church and Tower streets almost in the heart of downtown.*
>
> *That brings the number of names of Jamaica's children killed in under 12 years (2004-2016) and placed on the monument to 664. [The Gleaner, Sun. April 24, 2016]*

Since this article was published, several children have been murdered. When we see the number 664, we can think about 664 families grieving over such a heinous event that drastically separated them from their treasured loved one. Not to mention the friends, schoolmates, neighbours who don't know how to handle such tragedy.

The parents of murder victims face many unique struggles in their process of bereavement. A sense of loss of control is common, and the suddenness of the death is so overwhelming that, for a period of time, parents are often incapable of processing through the grief. For this group, dealing with spiritual beliefs, attitudes toward life, and general physical health may hold special importance.

[https://www.aamft.org/imis15/AAMFT/Content/Consumer _Updates/Grieving_the_Loss_of_A_Child.aspx]

This pain is indescribable and could last for a lifetime. Let's do the math. Consider the extended family, neighbours, school mates, Church associates, business / work associates who are impacted. Let's not forget the impact when it is being reported through the media. Whether the child was personally known to you or not, it grieves one's heart to hear of these senseless brutal killings of innocent children. But there is another category of loss.

What about the children reported missing and these kidnappings many times go unsolved? How does a parent live with not knowing whether their loved one is dead or alive? How does one bring closure and when you cannot, what...? How does one wrap their minds around the fact that their child could be alive and in some circumstances that might be driving them out of their minds, like child sex-slaves, human trafficking, etc. My heart truly goes out to those loved ones left behind, clueless! Their stories seem to sink into oblivion when the next news report emerges of another tragic loss of a child. That pain never seems to go away.

One of the realities that he/she has to live with is, I never got to say goodbye; I was not there to hold and comfort my child in his shock; I will never know what state he/she was in as the last breath was drawn or was taken away. Then, how do I deal with the one(s) who are responsible for the death/kidnapping? There is usually a strong sense of justice – they must pay for this! They will not get away with it. Sometimes the thirst for revenge drives especially the males to take action, e.g. taking up a weapon and going in search of the perpetrator(s). Whether they find the guilty ones or not, at least they took action to bring justice. This thing called real-ationships has made their pain possible because of opening their hearts to love in the first place but it has also left behind memories that are valuable, motivating, treasured, would not be given up for all the wealth in the world. It is because they have loved and were also loved why they are now filled with mixed emotions. The memories before the loss, remains priceless. Many look to God for comfort through the difficult months and years that follow. Some families even become closer as they are now more conscious of their mortality and the brevity of life. They form stronger real-ationships with those who remain.

How To Cope With Loss Through *Crime And Violence*

Forgiveness is Key. I could hear some immediate questions being asked. Forgiveness?! How can someone forgive another who did such a heinous act? Does the perpetrator(s) even deserve to live much less be forgiven? Who is going to pay for my loss and my pain? It is **not the letting go** of the bitterness that is going to **perpetuate the pain** and eventually destroy you/others **but holding on** to resentment and a thirst for revenge! Forgiveness, apart from being a divine command, is truly a healing balm for the soul. This is so since unforgiveness, as the story is told, is like a man who resents being slapped in his chest and straps dynamite to his chest and tells himself that he is going to teach the other man a lesson. So the dynamite strapped to him is him preparing to blow off the other man's hand when he comes to slap him in the chest. What would happen when this dynamite goes off? Who would suffer more injury and possible death? This is also a fact about unforgiveness. The person who is holding on to the grudge ends up in a worse pickle than the resented person. What is even more painful is oftentimes the one we are hating, sails away over the horizons into the sunset of great opportunities, pleasures and prosperity while the person heartsick with revenge, remains stuck in a life of failures because they are immobilized by thoughts and visions of revenge. Unforgiveness, bitterness and resentment are unfruitful. If these "trees" do bear fruit, they are blighted and fit only for the dump-heap.

Let me hasten to say that forgiveness is NOT being forced to accept a wrong action as if it was right and neither is it saying that justice must not be served in situations where persons are culpable. The Scriptures tell us that justice and righteousness are the foundation of God's Throne (Psalm 89:14). He is a God of justice! Joyce Meyer puts it this way:

> When an injustice happens, we want to be vindicated. A lot of times, people feel that if they forgive the person who hurt them, then they will continue to take advantage of them or not take responsibility for what they did wrong. And if we're honest, we'll admit that we usually want the person who hurt us to pay for what they did. We can't get past this until we get the revelation that only God can pay us back. He is our Vindicator and will heal and restore us if we will trust Him and forgive our enemies as He has told us to do. [http://www1.cbn.com/700club/do-yourself-favorforgive-interview-joyce-meyer]

Forgiveness is a **rational decision** to sincerely release from one's heart someone who has done us wrong and to resist the recalling of the person's deed(s). One has to pass the acid test of forgiveness. Are you willing to now sincerely BLESS the offender and wish him/her well? One person puts it this way, "Forgiveness is God's antidote for hate and the weapon against Satan – the one who accuses you before God" (Rev. 12:10f). The Bible helps us by stating it this way: "For the **weapons of our warfare** are **not carnal**, **but mighty** through **God** to the **pulling down of strongholds**." (2Corinthians 10:4 – KJV)

Counselling Can Be Helpful. Even as a professional counsellor, when my family faced the tragic loss of our son, we needed outside intervention. When you are the one wading through grief and confusion, you are like the surgeon, unable to perform surgery on your own body although you have the requisite knowledge and skills. No matter who we are and how much we know, when we experience an emotional tsunami, we need help, and we need to recognize that no man is an island. We might have to grapple with pride issues – what will people say or think when they see the counsellor or any another professional having to go in for counselling. One of the ways to deal with this is to ask, "Would I rather be a messed-up counsellor or an overcoming one in order to help others?" The truth is: I should believe in my own product and be willing to use it whenever it is applicable to me.

We were thankful for those who offered counsel at that time including Ministers of religion and a friend who was also a colleague in the counselling profession. One valuable counsel received was regarding how to assist our younger son, 2+ at the time, through his grief. It was about counselling grieving children. Qowayne, our deceased beloved and DeMario, our living beloved son were like two peas in a pod – they were playmates and growing as brothers. When DeMario took his first step, they were playing together on our wedding anniversary, and Qowayne was encouraging him to walk. "Come DeMario, come," was his common phrase to him whether encouraging him to do something, inviting him to play or just wanting to include him.

My grief was at its maximum but I was able to cope better when I realized the importance of now focusing on DeMario. We applied the guidelines given so that DeMario's loss could be minimized as much as possible. He was still at foundational stage and it was more important to help him to grow as wholesome as possible. We worked at keeping his schedule as close to consistent as it was before the loss. We kept him back in nursery with his friends rather than moving him into Kindergarten which could have been disruptive (another loss). We took him with us to many places that we had to visit, and he would always find some little friends to play with. God was faithful to always provide him with a young playmate even when we traveled with him half-way across the world. Even with a language barrier, somehow they were able to 'communicate' and play together. A few years later, when he was now cognitively able to process the death of his brother, another bout of grief came for him. We got counselling for him. We were told that he was too young at the time and could not remember much. What he was now grieving was the loss of the companionship that he could be now enjoying at home, if his brother was still around. It is amazing now, at the time of the writing of this book, how DeMario has become a more peaceful and settled teenager since his adopted sister, Jenene, has come to live with us. Even his relationship with me has become more demonstrative on his part. I believe having the company of a young person with whom he can relate has brought a sense of joy to his life.

At the time of our loss, I was recovering through counselling but I could discern the negative effect that the loss was having on my husband who loved him dearly. I felt as if I had lost my husband-friend too! He was still the faithful dutiful husband but emotionally he seemed to have gone into a cave. I, after about a year of much prayer, was now able to put on the "counsellor's hat" and assist in pulling him out of a pit of disappointment and other painful emotions. As a counsellor, I have had to help many out of painful scenarios that brought depression, disappointment and grief. Now it was in my family!

It is not a good sign if a counsellor is unable to be real and to accept that sometimes he/she might have to partake of his/her own medicine. What makes us real in counselling is that we can accept that as counsellors, we are really human and that we could also need a counsellor to take us through a specific season in our own lives. There is something that I jokingly say to my audience when encouraging them to go for counselling when needed and to stand against the cultural myth that only 'mad people go for counselling'. I tell them: "It is not those who are mad that go for counselling but those who don't want to become mad (don't want to become mentally ill)!" I have found that it is those who are quick to judge others who need to see a counsellor, who play the avoidance game of seeing a counsellor, when their "house is crashing all around them". Let's not judge and categorize persons who are in need of help and are humble enough to ask for it. I have never seen a physician doing surgery on himself, have you?

Walking With Your Hand in God's. If there is a time that you need to grab for God, it is when grief strikes. The feeling of loss is like sand shifting from under your feet. You find yourself sinking. Sometimes you neither know if you are coming or going. It can be a disruptive time in your life. The one Person that can be constant for you - unchangeable, unshakeable, and a truly firm foundation is God. You will need Him in the "midnight hour" when sleep is far from your eyes; the memories of your loved one comes flooding in; you are hungering and needing his/her touch; tormenting thoughts of regret, hopelessness and fear come all at once pounding in your head. You are unable to awaken your household, a pastor or a friend. What do you do?

The truth is that Jesus Christ is ALWAYS there. He comes close to us in our grief.

When Sickness or Tragedy Takes My Child

Some of you who have had to face this might even want to skip over this section. Why? It is just too painful. Yet I invite you to walk through with me as I too have had to journey through the loss of a child from the womb and one, though not biological, but it hurts the same. A few days ago, I met again the person who was doing the CPR on our son who died. She was the one holding him in her lap on the way to the hospital; the one who the hospital assumed initially was the mother because of her insistence that they jump into action and do something! She was also the one I saw leaving A&E, refusing to speak or making eye contact with me. It was her face that made me know that the end had come for him. It still stirs up some emotions that you have to swallow hard when listening, even when she spoke about how peaceful he looked – not the least sign of trauma, which was why she was insisting that he could not have passed. Thank you, Janice for your attempts at saving our son's life. We will not forget.

Sickness of a child is a tough one and watching a child suffer through terminal illness is unbearable. The first announcement of the condition of illness is devastating and the experience of watching that child deteriorate is beyond traumatic. If you are a person of faith, you pray every prayer in the book. If there are fifty types of prayer to pray, you find others! You bargain with God. Make vows you swear you are going to keep. Would pull out the last dollar; sell your house, car, etc. if you have to, in order to save that child's life. As bad as this experience is for you, it is far worse when there is sudden and tragic death. You often have one advantage over those who have had a sudden loss – the chance to prepare yourself and to say a last goodbye to that child.

Imagine, kissing your child who is leaving for ice-cream, expecting to see him home in a couple of hours. Those couple of hours only brought the news that your young son, 3 years old, is on his way to the hospital and they are hoping his life will be spared. What do you say? What do you pray? The wind is knocked out of you at those words. Imagine reaching the hospital and you take a look at your neighbour's face grimaced with pain. She is speechless and avoiding your eyes as you enter 'Emergency'. Then to see the lifeless body, those eyes that used to spark as soon as you walk in, now unresponsive! You somehow cannot predict what you will do in circumstances like these. Well, I climbed onto the bed on which he was lying. Somehow, it did not matter how I looked to anyone! I was crying out to God at that time.

Imagine going through the additional trauma of watching our other son, who was Q's 2 year-old playmate, who helped him to take his first steps in life. While at home, he was pointing to the floor and shouting that he wants to "go home". Imagine too, feeling the loss of your own husband, emotionally for almost two years following, because of the effect of this tragedy. The teacher who was home-schooling both our children abruptly ending the schooling of our younger son because the grief was too much for her. Not to mention Q's biological family and the other loved ones to whom we had to break the news. Broken hearts all around, including mine.

Then we had to deal with the "who was responsible" for his death. The way it happened no one could be sure who was liable. Without being able to point a finger at a specific person, one still has to go through dealing with the anger, rage, unforgiveness and possibly a desire for revenge. Someone was careless. We knew the accident could have been avoided!

We still carry much gratitude in our hearts for those who surrounded us with love and support. Our immediate families; the Church family; friends and strangers; my own Counselling Psychology students from the Seminary at which I was lecturing at the time who came as a large group and packed my living room. The hundreds of calls and cards. The surprise financial donations for us not to have to focus on the funeral expenses. I have detailed all of this because it is important that, at this time, there are real-lationships that you can count on for the type of support that you need. This is whether or not the loss of the child was through tragedy or illness. These real-ationships though are not formed overnight. It is as we pour our time, strength and resources into other people's lives. What goes around sure came right back around when we needed it the most! Not to mention the prayers!!! We felt those. The way I describe that season of our lives was like riding on a buoy in the middle of a vast ocean with heavy waves, but that buoy helps you to ride each wave and it never topples. You remain afloat in spite of the surrounding circumstances. God took us through, and the sincere prayers of caring persons sustained us.

We also had to be careful to keep our family life and activities, including within our marriage, as normal as possible. Life had to go on. Each family member still had needs to be met and God gave us the grace to do so. Although I felt that I had lost my husband for a while, emotionally, he still performed his husbandly duties, even with a broken heart. We kept things as stable as possible for DeMario, sending him to a school where he could be around friends; engaging him in other activities that were normal for him, especially where it meant that he would have playmates. Let me emphasize. This is critical for the child to get through his own grieving – keeping things as normal in his life as possible, the way they were before the death.

The parents who have had a tragic loss oftentimes would have preferred if they had the time to prepare themselves. They do not have the opportunity, painful as it is, to be with a sick child and you are being prepared by the medics, that he/she might not make it. The parents who go through tragic loss sometimes, have to live with regrets that the parent(s) of the terminally ill child have had a chance to fix by virtue of having time to face the reality of possible death. This is not in any means a belittling of the trauma too of caring for a very sick child – their grief starts from before death. They face frustrations, expenses, sometimes insensitive treatment of health practitioners in certain cultures; the time lost from work/business because of frequent hospital visits; the toll it can take on your body, mind and emotions and the disruption of normal family relationships. Imagine that after going through all of this, the child dies?

Again, as aforementioned, counselling can be very helpful and is often critical in helping you to pick up the pieces and move on. Death exposes our heart condition and general disposition and beliefs in life; our worldview. When we are confronted with self and even with the other side of our loved ones now exposed, we often need an objective ear and mind to help us understand what might be going on around us. What has changed within each one facing the loss? How can we work to eliminate the negative effects and build on the positives? How can we continue to build real-ationships with those who are still alive with purpose? How we can hold the Hand of the One Who knows best and does only good; never evil. Even informal counselling can help when we speak with others who have walked this road and have come out, not bitter but the better having walked through.

Where Is The Manual?

Getting back now to childbirth. So a baby is born into a family. Where are the instructions – the HOW TO RAISE THIS CHILD RIGHT step-by-step manual? As this child goes through life, while the parents constantly have to learn on the job, this child has to be taught how to relate to siblings, other relatives within and outside of the home, the neighbours, persons including adults and children at school and within their place of worship. This child will have to relate inside different educational institutions and social contexts. Most parents, I believe, deep down have to deal with the nagging question of, am I getting this thing right? Am I relating well to my child/children? Am I teaching them how to relate correctly to their peers, siblings, teachers and others who are in authority? Am I a good parent?!

Parents struggle with the "manual" they saw acted out in their parents' lives. Did their parent(s) get it right? Were they too strict or too lenient? How is raising children different now than it was then? Do the same rules apply and in the same way? Where is that manual? Who stole the guide?

Taking My Child Through the Early Years

Knowing fully well that these are foundational years brings some amount of trepidation – we are preparing them for life – to be the best partner, worker, citizen, and nation-builder. Just to be a great human-being that God and man would favour. Since there is no manual, we do have to learn from other people's experiences. Here are some principles that could help.

Laying a Proper Foundation

Nurturing. Without even studying Psychology, different cultures have discovered how important it is for the young to be adequately nurtured initially through bonding especially with parents and eventually through encouragement, support, training which includes disciplining of the child. Parenting feels like a full-time job so if you are working outside of the home, you come home to another job. Parents are there to help their children to prepare for the future. How the children are nurtured in their foundational years will make a big difference in how they perform in school and face the challenges at the various developmental stages and seasons of their lives. The lack of nurturing has produced ill-fitted abnormally adjusted adults who carry much "baggage" and make other people's lives miserable.

Personal Sacrifice. When I think of sacrifice, my own mother comes first to my mind. Growing up my mother was seemingly the epitome of sacrifice. Being a single parent, she sacrificed her life for us, denying herself of many things materially to ensure that we got a good education. She worked until nighttime in a drug store far away from home, to ensure that we had the best quality life that she could give us. This of course meant too that she was away from home a lot, and this had its consequences especially for me, the youngest of four and the only female. As I grew older, I learned to appreciate more this aspect.

I remember her telling me when I saw a picture of a male pen-friend who she never met and was from a developed country, that persons who knew of him were encouraging her to marry him and go overseas leaving us behind in order to make a better life for us. She was adamant that she would not leave her children behind. That did not work out. Parents should be selfless which means there are many things they have to forego especially in the first

36

eighteen years of their children's lives. My mother's example has affected me, not only in raising my own children but even in helping other children who might not have much in life, materially. It is a blessing to do so because I saw my mother do it naturally and with joy. Where I am now in life, has much to do with the sacrifices she made, even while I was in college.

Discipline. I am strongly of the belief that when it comes to the parent-child relationship, "discipline" is part of the definition of love. For some reason, these days when there is mention of the word discipline, the picture of abuse comes to mind. Children do not feel secure in life unless there are boundaries set for them. Parents who have thought otherwise have experienced the wrath of children who have been emotionally traumatized or severely damaged in life, because they were not taught that there are restrictions in the world, and that the world and relationships are not structured to meet their every need and fantasy. They had to come face-to-face with the harsh realities that militated against a narcissistic worldview. This was usually a hump in the road that overturned their vehicle of life and it went spinning several times down a precipice. The bangs and bruises, concussions and trauma that resulted, taught them in an unprepared for scenario, that in the script of life, he/she was not always the star player.

Many of us did not appreciate stern discipline while we were growing up. It is interesting however, to hear adults conversing, and reminiscing about how they were disciplined, only to be smiling and at that stage of life, appreciating the good that it did for them. They learnt later in life that they were not being abused and it did not "kill" them to experience boundaries set, privileges denied, the enforcement of rules, obedience and orderly conduct, which truly prepared them for the world at large.

TIME. This one I call **Taking Immediate Measures to Empower.** This takes time, in the natural. If we want to invest in our children to become the best human beings they can be, it does take time and attention. Attention to details of their lives. Attention to when they are hurting and not able to verbalize it. Attention to assist them with learning life skills, doing homework. Sometimes assisting them with chores so they learn what it is like to work as a team. It takes time to attend the PTA/HSA meetings, sporting and other events that our children are involved in or would just like to attend for recreation.

It also takes time to love and understand each child. It is amazing that you can have several children and no two are alike in temperament or personality. It takes time to relate to each one individually, and to ensure that each one's emotional tank is being filled. It takes time to clean up the bruises, bring comfort when they are disappointed. It takes quality time to care. Not rushed and distracted time which oftentimes leads us to make rash decisions that we later regret.

Accountability. I can recall one of my children when he fell down saying it was the other person who was nearby who was responsible for his fall. Sometimes, it was obvious that the other child was too far away to be even remotely connected. We had to teach him not to play the "blame game" but to take personal responsibility even for a fall. According to dictionary.com, 'accountability' is the state of being accountable, liable, or answerable. To be 'accountable' is to be 'subject to the obligation to report, explain, or justify something; responsible; answerable.

We must teach our child to take personal responsibility for their personal actions. This starts from very young. This also goes with disciplining. Our children have to learn, for example, if they leave their toys in the middle of the living room and someone slips on that toy and gets hurt, they have to take some of the blame, especially if they were taught not to leave their toys in that spot / to put away the toys in a secure place after they are finished playing with them. By this, they are taught that what we do and the choices that we make do have consequences not only for us but for others. When they disobey rules, they are going to have to be called to books and give an account to someone who is in authority, whether in the home, at school or later in life, in the workplace, etc.

Modeling. By the time children are in Kindergarten, they learn how to play 'Mummy' and 'Daddy'. It is amazing to watch children at play at this stage. You know who have daddies around them, leaving for work and telling the family goodbye. You know those who have mummies always in the kitchen, cooking and serving and the list goes on. Parents are modeling all the time whether they think about it or not. The days of "do as I say but not as I do" (a cop-out for bad behaviour while trying to instill good behaviour) are gone and should not have been in the first place. As parents, we should ask, "Is this the way that I want my son/daughter to emulate me? If I am the opposite sex parent, I need to ask, "Am I modeling the type of mate that I would want my child to choose?"

I am not here insinuating that we have to be perfect models. This could only be so if we are perfect people, and we are not. We can however, to the best of our abilities and with divine help, be the kind of human beings we would like our children to become. Or, if we realize that we are not being good examples, to be willing to humbly acknowledge to our children that we have not lived exemplary lives, and we do not want them to repeat the mistakes that we have made. After this, we can choose to repent of our wrong attitudes, beliefs and choices and begin to walk a new path, even asking the child, if he/she is old enough to help you to be accountable. They will help.

Building an Appropriate Value System. Have you ever stopped to ask yourself what are the things that you truly value – your personal value system? Let me give you a list of some possible core values:

Authenticity	Balance
Compassion	Courage
Community	Determination
Excellence	Friendship
Honesty	Industry
Integrity	Justice
Love	Loyalty
Peace	Religion
Personal Faith	Respect
Service	Trustworthiness
Wisdom	Work Ethics

Different social influences in a child's life will help to formulate a personal value system; however, the home is usually the first stop for the formation of the values that should form the child's foundation. It is the place that challenges or reinforces and solidifies the values that others attempt to teach to your child. These values usually deepen in the home especially if there is a solid family structure.

An article, *'How Parents Influence Early Moral Development'* reveals what research has shown:

A new study from the University of Chicago suggests that parents' sensitivity to both other people's feelings and to injustice may influence early moral development in their children... If we want our kids to be sensitive to justice— which I believe we do, if we want to live together in peace— and it turns out that the way that we handle or care for our kids can affect their sense of justice from very early on, then we will want to pay attention to that."

[https://greatergood.berkeley.edu/article/item/how_parents_in fluence_early_moral_development]

In another article, *'Importance of Family Values'* by Marcelina Hardy, she writes:

Family values influence the decisions people make both within the family structure and outside of it. Making a decision about important topics can be difficult, and people may feel helpless if they don't know which way to proceed. Therefore, having solid family values helps people make the right decisions in life...Parenting can be a challenge and with all of the world's influences, it can be downright scary. Knowing what you believe in as a parent and what you want for your children will help you raise them to be responsible and conscientious adults. [family.lovetoknow.com]

Parents must in this postmodern culture resist the lure of society to allow our children to decide what they want to believe, think, fashion, and model. We are not called to brow-beat children into thinking or doing things the way we want them to but we do have a responsibility to obey an important principle of Scripture which has not failed our fore-parents. We need to, "Train up a child in the way he should go: and when he is old, he will not depart from it." (Proverbs 22:6 – KJV)

Having a Welcoming Home Environment. I was in dialogue recently with a young adult who said she did not feel welcomed in her home while growing up. Wow! What a feeling that must have been for a youth. Even as adults, if we don't feel welcome in our home environment, we don't want to be there; we become a recluse; we seem to "disappear" psychologically into thin air, the moment we arrive home. Can you imagine what this could do to a child? A child needs a happy home; a secure place where he/she can be the person who God created them to be. A place to feel safe from what is sometimes to them, "a harsh cruel world" where there is not much safety and security for the children.

Annabelle, a past counsellee, has allowed me to share her story with permission. Her name has been changed for purposes of anonymity. She decided to share under the headings of her thoughts, feelings, sensations, reactions and ideal response (upon retrospection). This is often used with my clients to help them to analyze their responses especially in situations of conflict or trauma.

Annabelle's Story: I Felt Unwelcomed in my Own Home

These are some of the thoughts, feelings, sensations and reactions I had as I felt unwelcomed in my own home mainly because of my mother who should have been my confidant and support emotionally, even though she was there financially and otherwise, I felt the gap where it mattered most.

My Thoughts:

- I needed my own space because in that way I won't be a bother to anyone

- Having my own space is the only way I can have my peace of mind

- My mother doesn't even know her own daughter

- If I think I excelled at something, rather than giving a compliment then giving the negative feedback, she always gave negative feedback, so I thought it was her nature to just always find fault

- Even though she was there to ensure we got ahead in life, which I wonder too if it's because that makes parents look good too, if their children excel, it is the only thing I really could give her credit for. BUT there was a longing for affection and a safe zone which never came. After the teenage years I stopped looking for it from her and began looking outside.

My Feelings:

- I felt like I could not do things well enough to please my mother and that everything was followed with a criticism, so I felt like I could not do anything well enough for her.

- I felt manipulated and like I had to do what the other person wanted me to do in their timing or otherwise it would be a problem. It was as if a request was made and you didn't respond in her timing, she made you feel like you were of no help or if it was housework for example that you were lazy. It's almost like I was always placed in a position where I felt like I had to set back myself in order to meet her demand.

- I felt there was no *me-time* when she was around; I felt uneasy

- I felt judged wrongfully rather than feeling like she was trying to understand me and lovingly helping me to be a better person.

- I felt stifled like I couldn't genuinely express how I truly felt or give my opinion about things

- I felt like I wasn't heard but all I said was used against me in some cases at another time. When visitors came to the house, I didn't want to be around because in some instances thought she deliberately used that opportunity to get me to do something she wanted done her way and embarrass me hence my reason for not wanting to be around.

Sensations

- Unrelaxed within my body when in her presence. My body would feel tense when she was there.

My Reactions

- I felt for my peace of mind I needed to avoid her so I remained in places of the house where I could do that or used activities outside the home as a getaway. I am not good at pretending so if visitors come and things are not right between me and her, I would just stay away to avoid being forced to put on a show.

- I refrained from sharing very personal things with her and related mainly on a social level or a need to basis

- I diarized my thoughts rather than sharing them or I internalized them

- I shared more personal things with my Dad because he was a different person

- I slept over at friends' and family houses which was always a welcomed change, breath of fresh air as I felt non-judgmental interactions with the friends I had

- I blocked my mind to her opinions and became more open to those of older friends and people who showed that they had my best interest at heart

Ideal Response

> In retrospect, what would I do differently in terms of response? During counselling, with the advice of my counsellor, I attempted to reach out and communicate my feelings and how certain behaviours were affecting me but was unsuccessful and I didn't know what else to do.

One of the things, as a counsellor, I attempted to help Annabelle to do was to be real. To be honest with herself by identifying what she was truly experiencing at the time and to also be real with her mother, who was still alive. This is one way to avoid having any regrets after people die. Regretting that situations were not confronted, and an attempt was not made to resolve issues and bring closure. Annabelle's freedom came, not in "changing her mother", since that was not in her power to do so, but in expressing some of those thoughts and emotions which were locked up for years. She could move on with her life as a result. The conflicts from her youth could be faced maturely and she could make certain decisions to move on.

Many parents might not have an Annabelle returning to tell them where they might have missed it. Having read Annabelle's story, and some pointers that will be shared in this section, it would be helpful to us and our relationship with our children (even if they are now adults), to revisit, reassess, own any mistakes and misunderstandings and seek to bring clarity and apologize where necessary, so you and your children can have a better real-ationship going forward. So what are some of the things that many parents miss when dealing with their teens.

Keeping It Real For The Testing Tremendous Teen

There are two developmental stages in a child's life that parents absolutely dread. It is what is usually dubbed the "Terrible Twos" and the "Troubled Teens". Each brings out a different set of conflicts in the home and within the parents. The latter, because the child is bigger, even in stature, brings with it more toe-to-toe confrontations. I have heard of fist-fights and physical tussling between parents and children at this stage; running away from home – parent or child; closed spirits to each other, leading to a serious breakdown in future relationship between them. If there is a time when parents feel that they are facing competition with the outside world; that what friends and peers say count more than all they have taught and reinforced over the years; that they could be losing their child to weird fashions and customs; to drugs and illicit lifestyles, it is during the teen years.

There are some common issues that usually cause much conflict in the home – non-conformity to rules laid out; bad school performance and the impact it has on the child's future – how this affects choice of schools/colleges/scholarships; the child's choice of friends, social gatherings and activities that are not in keeping with the family's value system; how discipline is handled by both child and parent and the nature of the relationship even prior to this stage of life. This can be a stage that could have one tearing out his/her hair or trusting God like you have never done to take you to safe landing in this, for most families, tumultuous season. This is when all the "masks" fall off. Those sweet and gentle parents begin to have thoughts of physically assaulting their teen; dreams of a home without their once treasured offspring; abusive words having to be fought back in the mind; images of the police visiting their home for one reason or another. This is not an easy time! Not only do parents have these thoughts but to their own shock, some actually act them out and later condemn themselves for not having more self-control; for not taking the upper road and doing the better that they know; for not acting with the maturity with which they prided themselves. Here are some guidelines, while you desire to keep it real, you will find helpful.

How Parents Can Cope at These Times

Ensure that Rules are FAIR and Consequences Clear. Many times our teens will cry out "Injustice" is being done. One way to avoid or disclaim this utterance is to sit with the teen beforehand and lay out the rules, ensuring that each party understands what is expected and what are the rewards and penalties. At that stage, the parents should be open to discussing with their adolescent the system of rewards and punishment. It is a great idea to involve the child in setting up this system by even asking, what do you think would be fair "rewards" for upholding and observing rules and just "penalties" for such-and-such an infraction. You would be amazed how well they do, if you give guidelines.

Spend Quality T.I.M.E. With Them. It has often been said that for the child, love is spelt TIME. This is speaking of literal time or quality time needed by the child with you. This is also true for the Teen. I can already hear the reaction, "But he/she no longer wants me around. They are forever locked inside their room." This may be true but they still need to *know* that you are there; you are around when they need you and they will. It is so hard to deal with this stage of "rejection" which causes pain, coming from one's teen, but at the end of the day, they would go to pieces if they lost you! I would like to use the acronym, T.I.M.E. to break down some of the critical things that parents must do in order to keep that relationship with their teens, even if the relationship is rocky.

> ➤ *T – Teaching using a more engaging than lecturing approach*. At this stage they truly begin to tune-out the lecturing that they have heard all their lives. They check-out! This calls for us being more creative and innovative and with God's help and wisdom, we can do it. Part of this engagement might mean instead of straight instructions, we invite, throw out questions, what if scenarios – the kinds of things that will make them think for themselves and help to come up with solutions, developing their problem-solving skills. Sometimes

we can allow them to help set their consequences that will be meted out for wrong choices and unacceptable behaviour / violation of rules. This of course calls for a certain level of communication which does take time.

➢ *I – Identifying with their failings than disconnecting when disappointed.* One of the worst scenarios that a parent can face is watching his/her child making the same mistakes that they themselves have made and have warned them not to make. These are the horrendous moments parents try to avoid. If teenage pregnancy devastated a parent and shattered the dreams of his/her own parents, that nightmare, this parent does not want to relive through his/her own child. Yet, if this occurs, this is the time that he/she needs you the most. They don't need their also frightened friends advising them to take risky or ungodly steps.

Sometimes this very fear keeps us from being real with our offspring. We do not often want to share our weaknesses of the past and how we blundered – behaved like we "hit our heads" and acted foolishly. It takes great humility to sit before a child and to say, "I blew it when I was growing up. I did thus and thus and paid the consequences, some of which might be affecting you right now and I want to spare you the trauma." The truth is, if we have opted to have real-ationships, and to remain real within ourselves and stay in touch with what we experienced at their age, we would be better able to remain connected emotionally with them, even when disappointed. The trouble comes when either we had never experienced the upheavals of adolescence (we were either unique, sheltered or spared certain exposure), or we moved on and did not properly process those mixed up moods and attitudes we experienced with our parents and within other relationships while growing up.

The best thing we can do for our teens, young adult children, is not to disconnect. Sometimes it is only in the strength of the Lord that we can remain connected especially if we are traumatized by their actions, including their rejection of us and the principles for which we stand. It becomes even harder when we too have to painfully face the consequences of their wrong choices.

> *M – Manage your home but with a different style of leadership.* It's amazing how we can get together with workers or with a Management Team in the workplace to change our style of Management

because it is no longer working or producing the required results, yet we are stumped when it comes to emotional relationships. We must examine, especially as our children are going through different developmental stages our leadership style within the home.

As our son became a teen and puberty set in, we realized that the way we brought correction into his life had to change. Our standards of what was wrong and right did not change. We did not enter into an integrity crisis. What changed was our approach. Since he is male, I stepped back somewhat and allowed his father to take on most of the role of a disciplinarian. There is something that men understand about themselves and thus about raising a son. Some take it to the extreme of becoming harsh and abusive. This is not what I am addressing here. It is the manner that they address the male, man-to-man. It is watching how a son responds to a male's command differently. For me as a female, it is not wanting to have an "up in his face" kind of approach that is combative, a very tempting tactic especially when a parent feels she is not being heard by the adolescent. This is important because as female parents/guardians, we have to be cognizant of the fact that we are modeling what a female should be and the type of woman they should choose for a life partner. Oh yes, every day we are modeling this and if we behave like a virago, and our son brings home one that he is dating, who is to blame?

"A body of psychological research reveals that our earliest relationships, especially with our mother, not only influence how we are able to connect to others as adults—in romantic and other contexts— but also create internalized scripts or working models of how relationships work."

Briefly, securely attached children, with loving and consistently attuned mothers grow up to be adults who see themselves positively, are comfortable seeking out close relationships and depending on others, and don't worry about being alone or being rejected."

[https://www.psychologytoday.com/blog]

This is also true of a father with his daughter. Children tend to choose similar personalities/temperaments to their opposite gender parent. Research has demonstrated this. An Empirical Test of the Psychoanalytic Theory of Mate Selection done by Glenn Geher, Western

Oregon University and Kathleen P. Bauman, Pacific University, informs us about this:

"Analyses revealed that participants perceived their partners (and ideal partners) as similar to their parents (both same and opposite-sex) at above chance levels. However, actual similarity between parents and partners existed much less than this perceived similarity. For some personality dimensions, partners were actually similar to opposite-sex parents. No significant similarity between partners and same-sex parents was found." *[http://www2.newpaltz.edu/~geherg/POSTER1.html .]*

What counsellors have found to be troubling is how the cycle of abuse continues through the generations even based on this theory. Children, who have literally hated their abusive parent, have either become abusers themselves and/or hitched up with abusive partners. So how we grow and discipline our children is setting them for life, choosing life partners and how they too will relate within their new family.

Growing up being surrounded by physical and verbal abuse I realized later predisposed me to choose earlier in my life, opposite to my desire, a significant other who was abusive. The strange thing is that I had never liked rough treatment. When I ended up in a relationship where the individual was abusive, I was shocked at myself. The truth is, I did not have a father in the home to model to me what a female should expect in a relationship. The male-female relationships that were around me were unhealthy and not impressive – much abuse, infidelity, domestic violence. It is indeed important to have in your home model parents or parent-substitutes as, whether we like it or not, we do embrace later on in life, much of what is familiar to us in our growing up years. Thank God for my husband who models in our home what God intended for male-female relationships. I have thought to myself: "If my son does not treat women well, it will certainly not be because he did not have an excellent role model.

➤ **E – Endear yourself to their friends so you will know what is happening.** One of the last things parents want to do is to relate to friends of their children that they are naturally repulsed by. They don't usually want them inside their homes/space. Yet, by not allowing them into our space, we deny ourselves the privilege of knowing what is happening in their lives and in their association with our child/ren. Apart from just wanting to have knowledge of what they are up to, it provides the opportunity for us to influence their friends in a positive way. Some of their school mates will be coming from very dysfunctional homes and do need mature stable adults to help them to stabilize their own lives. I will never forget the difference of the adults (parents of my friends) while I was growing up. One set was open to me and gave me guidance along the way which I heeded, while another set, rejected me because of the fact that I was not in their social class. I grew up in the ghetto (inner-city). Some of this rejection I knew by experience (I overheard conversations which explained why I was treated unkindly) and some I knew even recently while writing this book. A past classmate and friend messaged me, apologizing on behalf of her now deceased mother. I will quote from her message (I have her permission to do so) since this could help some adult/parent reading this book. She wrote:

"My mother passed away .... My mother, while she was alive, was such a snob and I was rebellious. She didn't want me associating with you because of where you lived but I found a friend in you because of who you were..... You were aware of it because we would walk

home together and as soon as we got near enough to my home we went our separate ways.

So sorry Maria. With that I too learned a valuable lesson. You can't predict a child's future based on the parent's life. It is no fault of the child that they are in the situation in which they find themself. A real caring adult should try to nurture, not ridicule that child. I would like to apologize for my mother's behavior. It has bothered me all these years and I am glad that I have found you so that I can apologize. I only wish that she was alive to see the wonderful child of God that you are. Please keep up the good work. (KW)

I was very surprised by these messages in our chat. I had moved on and had been restored emotionally. I was even more surprised that for decades she waited on an opportunity to fix this, although it was not her fault or doing. I know, from being an intercessor, the role of standing-in-the-gap to apologize on behalf of another. I have seen how effective it is in the counselling room and could appreciate the role that KW was now playing.

The reality is that all of us as adults might need to do some soul-searching. I wonder if we too, as adults, need to apologize to some children; need to ask God's forgiveness for our snotty attitude; need to correct in our children, the notion we have reinforced, that they are superior or inferior to other people's children. The truth is, let's get real, if we have to strive by viewing ourselves/our children as being superior to others, or as underdogs and victims, it only points to feelings of inferiority and deep insecurities within us as adults! If the only way we can feel good about ourselves is to look down on others, then we have some homework to do. We have to get real and confess to ourselves that we know deep inside that "we are not all that" and seek counsel to fix what is broken. If we have embraced the myth that humility is behaving like victims, then we need to be transformed by the renewing of our minds.

Life is so strange and God, not us, has the handle on how even our children and other people's children will turn out. We should wish and encourage as much as we can, all children to end up well. We should wish for all children to pass their exams; not just ours. We should want to see all children succeed and become great models in life; not just our children. We should pray not only for our own children but for others who might not have anyone to pray specifically for them.

Could we be called in life to be that "missing guide" for a wayward child? Could we be an answer to prayer, out of a deep cry from that child to God, for someone to care and assist him/her when parents are unable or unwilling to do so? Could what has been a troublesome experience of some parents be our outcome – a child that was not our own but to whom we extended a heart of compassion, ended up being our help in sickness, aid when needed or companion in old age, when our own children have sailed away in the sunset.

My Child Is Dating/*Courting?*

So we are able to get them through nursery to High School. It seems like a quick succession of events and various relationships, and soon the parents are being introduced to another real-ationship that can change all of their lives – a possible spouse for their child. To this spouse they will have to adjust themselves, checking their own standards and prejudices, wondering if they or their offspring is ready for such a step in life. Introduced in their lives, is another set of relationships, the potential spouse's family. Things are great if they have a special liking or love for their offspring's new attachment(s) and vice-versa. But what if this is not the case? How do they deal with any hint of disagreement with their child's choice which could negatively affect even the most solid parent-child relationship? They are called upon to carefully and wisely meander their way through their own thoughts and emotions surrounding this choice that they cannot make for their treasured child. The following chapter will look in more depth at this possible dilemma.

When a union develops between their child and his/her spouse, if parents are in agreement they can joyfully welcome a "daughter" or "son" into their family. If it is someone they are proud of, and proud to have their photo displayed in their home or at work, then all power to them. But what if they are not at peace about his/her selection? Now they are "compelled" to attend a wedding, invite a not favourite daughter/son-in-law to special family functions; deal with grand-children that may exhibit more of the genes of the "unwelcomed" in-law. They have to choose to relate to their child's choice of intimate relationship. This may be for the rest of their existence on earth. Frightening?

It is amazing how each entrance of a different relationship in one individual's life can transform that person positively or negatively, and can impact those around with whom he/she relates. There are no neutral relationships within the sphere of family, friendships or fraternities. Each person is being influenced and impacted in some way. Decisions are being made within each context that will change the course of other people's existence in one way or another. Hopefully this influence is for good, because whether or not, a whole family, school, community, institution, organization and nation can be changed for a lifetime by one life and one type of relationship. Have you ever seen a life that is overtaken by drugs or crime and how all of the abovementioned areas pay a price in one way or another? How persons who come into contact with this individual sometimes wish that either they or the individual was dead – not having to experience this painful journey in life. The family, for their own emotional health, have to keep it real with this individual, recognizing the extent to which his/her choices are impacting the welfare of the family unit. Sometimes it gets to crisis proportion leading to a separation from the one with the deviant behaviour.

Now that your child is dating or courting, what should a parent expect? What can a parent do to make this new encounter not a traumatic one for their children and the entire family? I believe the first stop is to look at how the relationship between them as parents can and might have affected how the child has learned within the home to relate to the opposite sex. Various researches have shown that what parents model in the home, in their relationship, does affect their children's perspective on how to relate in an intimate relationship in adulthood.

Sacha Strebe, [**https://www.mydomaine.com/author/sacha-strebe**] in an article, "6 Ways the Relationship With Your Parents Affects Your Love Life Later On" wrote:

> ___Modern dating___ *is fraught with challenges in this fast-paced, technology-fueled world, but no matter how chaotic our schedules are or what obstacles life throws in our path, we all drop everything in the name of love.... But how you give and receive it is greatly influenced and shaped by one or two very important people in your life: your parents. In fact, Rebecca Bergen, Ph.D., licensed clinical psychologist and co-owner of **Bergen Counseling Center** in Chicago, told MyDomaine that our first experience with this emotion is with our parents, and those early years set the bar for how we see, give, and*

*receive love, and what we want out of **relationships** later in our lives. [https://www.mydomaine.com/relationship-with-parents]*

Bergen lists some ways that we can raise our children to enhance their future relationships.

- Be a model for who you want them to be in the way you express love, anger, hurt, joy, etc., both toward them but also toward your partner.

- Teach them how to express their feelings starting early.

- Show them unconditional love with boundaries for behavior.

[https://www.mydomaine.com/relationship-with-parents]

Parents have to live within the home with a conscious knowledge that whatever they do, even outside of the home, impacts on their children. How faithful they are to their spouse; how they handle matters of integrity – money, other relationships, work, etc. all impact on how well adjusted their children will be in the future.

The following chapter will give some guidelines parents can give for dating and courtship.

Image by Free Photos from Pixabay

CHAPTER TWO

ATTACHED: MALE – FEMALE RELATIONSHIPS

"Men most often know what they want, yet they are not always sure how they feel. Women most often know how they feel, yet they may not always know what they want." — <u>Ken Poirot</u>

S o they are growing up. In the pre-adolescence years, girls stick to girls because boys are too rough; the boys don't want the girls on their team because they are too soft and will let them lose the match. Then, before the parents could even notice the transition, the tables turn and the "attractions" begin. Each gender is seeing the other through new pairs of glasses. The afore-avoided specie is now deemed as cute, and they are having a "crush" on each other. The little time that parents were having with their children is now being invaded by text messages from this once rejected specie. Their son/daughter cannot resist responding, even in the middle of conversations with the parents, they are texting/answering that call. This relationship becomes more important to them now. What their peers think and in particular, what that party thinks of them, is more critical than what parents think. The dress code changes and sometimes some strange behaviours occur, like sneaking out of the house or sneaking things out of the home that they should not be. This is all being done for their new "friend" or simply to impress.

This relationship seems the "realest" to them now. Other relationships are submerged in the background. Parents are confused; younger siblings are complaining; teachers are appalled at the drastic fall in grades; the "in love" son/daughter is also experiencing muddled emotions. They had never felt this way before and are not quite sure what to do with these new exciting but sometimes disturbing emotions. Their hormones are rushing around within them like a cyclone and they are not quite sure how to deal with this tempest.

In keeping it real, what can parents/guardians/teachers do to help the child who might now be betwixt and between being a teen and a young adult?

My Child is Dating – "In Love"

For some parents, this is a joke. It brings healthy laughter to the dinner table. To others however, it's the parents worse nightmare and for different reasons. (a) If they always wanted a "baby", the stark reality of their child no longer being a baby, creates some emotional upset within them. (b) The fear of losing this precious relationship. A fear that as their child becomes attached to someone else, they might become less attached to the parent(s) and thus to home. (c) The "Empty-nest syndrome" - a feeling of loneliness or sadness that occurs among parents after children grow up and leave home. The feeling that they are approaching this stage of life where their child might be planning to move away from home can be frightening and disheartening.

This we know is a natural stage of life and should even be encouraged, yet how we prepare ourselves to face this music will make a difference when the time comes. This stage needs to happen for generativity. How then should we respond to this new phase? By this time, if we have been real in our relationships with our children, we should be talking openly and honestly about sexuality. We should have been teaching them about relationships and about developing healthy relationships with the opposite sex. We should have been establishing dating guidelines with them – appropriate age to date, individual versus group dating, acceptable behaviour while on a date, safe places to be on a date, etc. If you have not, it is not too late. Read on.

Talking About Sex and Sexuality

For some parents/guardians, this is an uncomfortable time. Depending on their own temperament, training and background, they could find themselves avoiding these issues and hoping that school will be the transmitter of this knowledge. The risk we take is that it might be school, but not in the sense of sensible teaching in the classroom, but by friends who know just as little or less. It will be the old adage of "the blind leading the blind". When the ignorant is leading the ignorant some myths are usually passed along which can be indelibly etched in the child's mind. Unless someone of influence through oral or written discourse corrects this quickly, such a child could end up building his/her life and relationships on a false foundation. The end results are usually devastating!

Once we are preparing to have children, we should prepare ourselves for the difficult tasks we must be willing to undertake in helping them to grow up. To give talks on puberty, including body changes, hormonal changes, mood swings, having the desire for sexual contact, minds being now preoccupied with thoughts of intimate relationships, the strong desire to please one's peers, dealing with distractions, technology and otherwise, the need for further autonomy and taking on more responsibility.

If you find yourself struggling to approach these topics, then you could speak with a friend/counsellor but try not to avoid this critical preparation for them. If you have been honestly relating to your child before puberty, then you should be able to flow into this conversation. Approach it making it as comfortable for you and child as possible. Some find it easier to use visual aids, e.g. dolls, pictures. Some prefer to ask questions to find out how much the child already knows and they fill in the blanks. Some parents do it together while others speak to the same sex child. For my own son, his Dad took him out to eat somewhere and while eating, they had "man talk". Because of the openness in relating that my son and I have developed since he could speak, he finds it easy to express especially pain to me. He will tell me about any part of his body that is hurting, where there is an issue and he might need medication. At times it was a bit embarrassing when I had to look at a rash on his penis but I am his Mom. He is also not afraid to tell us when he feels things intensely – good, bad or indifferent. Sometimes when he is being very honest about his feelings, especially when he is upset, I have to remind myself that this "being real about what we feel" was cultivated in our home and now he does not feel the need to hide. What we teach while this is going on is how to listen to each other. That he also needs to listen to how others feel too. Phew! Sometimes, this is a tall order and is easier said than done.

Maybe I have been more encouraged to be open with children because much of what I learnt about sex and sexuality was at school and not from adults around me who learnt and developed many myths about the topic on the streets. It was some great school teachers that I had, like the late Rosemarie Vernon, who was a former pre-High School teacher but remained close to me during my High School years, guiding me re male-female relationships. She was such a straightforward person that she got me to reveal my "secret boyfriend" when I was in High school. Her openness and guidance is remembered with much gratitude. She was one of those who positively impacted my early years as she referred to me as "the daughter I never had". I will share some guidelines for those parents who might be struggling, like my Mom might have been, to share with their children, the bare facts-of-life.

Let me share an account with you from one of my previous clients. The Story of a Once Confused Young Client [used by permission]. The client asked to title this story: **"Victory Testimony"**

The door opened with masturbation and then came other challenges such as unnatural affection for the same sex. Satan wanted me to believe that masturbation was only a release but in reality in the long run it brought on guilt, unhappiness, shame and more struggles.

I silently cried to the Lord daily telling him I am sorry for opening that door from my early teens when I started going through puberty. I got my deliverance directly from the Lord during my late teenage years as one day I realized that things that use to evoke certain unnatural sexual feelings were no longer doing so, and I realized the Lord finally heard my daily cry, because growing up in the church I knew these desires were not of Him.

One thing I found was that I could also empathize with someone else who was having the struggle with unnatural same-sex attraction and could tell him that he should cry out to the Lord and He will surely deliver. I didn't judge that boy because I myself went through the same struggle. Now, I am also less judgmental of people when they fall into sin because I tell myself if it was me that was facing their circumstances I don't know what I would have done, but only for the grace of God I didn't sink deeper and deeper into sin.

The struggle with masturbation left for a while in my late teens and re-surfaced in my late 20's when I started entertaining thoughts that there are no prospects to get married in the short run as I wasn't currently dating anyone and so marriage was in the distant future. This thought was reinforced because friends around me were getting married or finding significant others and had prospects of marriage. I therefore believed the lies of Satan that masturbation was the only release for now and again I became trapped giving into this temptation. Again, I started crying out to the Lord to break me free from it.

One day some people in a Christian meeting prayed for me and afterwards I felt free. Whilst the struggle came now and then after that, it was getting less and less and I also didn't enjoy it anymore when I did it occasionally. As a matter of fact I felt like when I gave in it was me feeling like it would satisfy my urges even though I felt the strength of the Lord to resist the temptation. It was my curious mind wanting to experience sex again but it wasn't like in the past where the overwhelming feeling came and I couldn't find the strength to resist. In addition to that the Lord kept reminding me of how opening the door during the teenage years created other sexual struggles and unhappiness.

On the practical side, I am accountable to a more spiritually mature person than myself who consistently reminds me that I should remain pure and holy. That person knows when I have fallen in sin because they discern where I am in my spiritual life. Satan only comes to steal, kill and destroy and he makes sin look very attractive until you get deep into it you realize that it isn't what he made it out to be after all. You feel let down. There is really only one source of true joy and fulfillment which I once knew and that is JESUS CHRIST! Everything else is bonus in our lives but they can't give us everlasting never-failing joy. Now I strive to be there – let Jesus be the centre of my joy. In spite of our circumstances and what is happening around us He can make us smile in the midst of it.

Having had to work with this client over a period of time to deal with sexuality issues, conflicts and confusion, they were able to have a sense of victory in being able to manage urges that seemed to dominate their life. As reported, it did not happen all at once and as implied, these urges, the natural ones, remained but were now being subjected to the person's control. My client no longer felt like a victim but a victor.

Some guidelines, adapted from an article, *Talking With Kids Openly and Honestly About Sexuality*, by Michael McGee, C.S.T., Vice President for Education, Planned Parenthood Federation of America:

Put aside fear or just do it afraid, as long as we do it. McGee wrote: "sexuality is ... an essential, lifelong aspect of being human, and ... is celebrated with respect, openness, and mutuality. ... sex and sexuality are good and positive aspects of life. So how does this translate into something parents can support without encouraging early or inappropriate sexual behavior?"

http://www.advocatesforyouth.org/parents

McGee, I believe touches on a key aspect – *fear*! Many times we don't want to introduce the topic of sexuality because we fear that we might be opening up "a can of worms"; we might be awakening the child to a consciousness of aspects of himself that he was not aware of prior to the talk and that this could lead to new behaviour that the child is not ready for. If, especially Christian parents will be real with themselves on this topic, many see it as taboo, in the same way that to many, sex is believed to be only for procreation. If there is a religious block then we won't want to discuss this topic with anyone, and especially not with children. Sex and sexuality however, was God's idea. Remember, if we don't teach them openly the right way to understand and approach their sexuality, others could easily mislead them. We only have to ensure that our talks are age-appropriate. McGee wrote:

By telling the truth. Too often, when we talk with young people, we talk about the dangers of sexual behavior, and we leave out the positive feelings. Every adolescent who has had a "crush" knows the pleasurable feelings that come with having an intense attraction to someone. Young people need to hear from us, the caring adults in their lives, about the pleasure as well as the responsibility of sexuality.

[http://www.advocatesforyouth.org/parents]

One of the notions that we have to undo, especially in a strongly Christian culture, is the myth that pleasure is of the devil and God wants us to live boring lives, without the enjoyment of an intimate relationship with the opposite sex. God created us to have pleasure but in the right context. Ps 16:11 – "Thou wilt show me the path of life: In thy presence is fullness of joy; In thy right hand there are pleasures for evermore." (ASV) Although this has changed very much over the past two decades, there are middle-aged and older persons, who still, by attitude, words and actions, attempt to stir up condemnation in persons who want to have a pleasurable intimate relationship in the context of marriage. Let's be real. Sex is not only about procreation! If so, after we had our children, God would have shut down our sexual desires and responses.

McGee also makes reference to "the experience of "skin hunger"—the need to be touched, held, or caressed. This pleasurable aspect of sexuality is critical to normal and healthy development." I can remember experiencing this "skin hunger" from as little as seven years old when I became conscious of the "pleasures" of being touched. How I discovered this pleasure was unfortunate, as it was through an adult inappropriately touching me. This was followed by other adults, one in my neighbourhood, who pretended to want to "parent" me and to love me as a child but were merely consuming their own lusts upon me. **I incorrectly** learnt at a very young age, that there was something "dirty" about the genitals. That sex and sexuality was about hiding, as the adults who molested me always did so in hiding and not wanting me to reveal their inappropriate touch to my mother (I grew up in a single-parent home) or siblings. I also incorrectly learnt that this type of touch could come from a stranger, neighbour, anyone who could access you to take advantage of you. It was only years later, thank God it was in my teens, that I learnt about the beauty of love real-ationships and God's gift of intimacy that He gave to mankind to procreate and to enjoy each other in an atmosphere of commitment.

McGee points out that:

Young children who touch their genitals do so because it feels good. They don't fantasize about sexual things at this age. We need to remember not to overreact to our children's early genital exploration.

[http://www.advocatesforyouth.org/parents]

Even reading this statement by him, I can feel older persons reacting, surprised at his perspective and some might even think that this is a liberal and dangerous approach to children touching their own genitals. Whereas I believe that at every stage and with various actions, children need to be guided about appropriate and inappropriate touch, even when they touch their own bodies, I do believe that there is a necessary caution here re our approach. Shaming, embarrassing, punishing small children for example, who walk around the house with their hand in their pants is doing more damage than good to the child. We can gently guide the child and help him/her to break such a habit without making the child feel dirty or sinful. Older children who do this, if they are not challenged (have a disability), can be strongly corrected but even with them, adults need to ensure that we are not sending a wrong message – that pleasure is evil; sex is dirty; he/she is abominable for doing such an act.

This is the time when private talks between parents and their pre or adolescent children must take place and sometimes frequently. The children might be questioning some of the changes and experiences in their own body. I am smiling while writing, as I am recalling insisting at age eleven that my mother take me to the doctor. I was having pain in especially one of my breasts. Of course the doctor sent us away with no medication but a smile on his face – I was entering puberty! Alarm did come though, and I panicked when I had my first period. I had no one at home to talk to since menstruation was never a subject discussed with me in the home. I knew enough about buying and using sanitary pads from the illustrations given by the nurse at my school. I however felt that it had to be top secret although my best-friend and I promised each other that we would tell the other when it happened. I told no one. I hid the pads until one day my mother saw an open package. That's when I knew my "secret" was out. If there was no discussion in the home about menstruation then you know that there was absolutely no discussion about hormonal changes, natural sexual feelings and inappropriate touch.

Boys in particular need much attention at this point. Knowing how to manage some normal occurrences like erections, having "wet dreams", experiencing voice change, etc. This is around the time when male-female attractions take place and parents need to be proactive in guiding them about the issues of attractions, having crushes, having sexual desires, natural discharges and even about perversion in their attraction. A critical part of the discussion must be about setting boundaries for their own sexual behaviour and reactions to those of the same and opposite sex. They must be taught how to respect themselves and others in their interactions. Both genders must be taught how to respect each other and not to view others as objects and outlets for their sexual urges. They need to be taught the threshold not to cross in order to avoid early sexual activities. Both sexes (not just the girls) need to be taught responsible sexual behaviour and ways in which they can maintain integrity from an early age. Both genders need to be taught that virginity is a blessing and abstinence is not a curse. This is difficult to teach in a very permissive culture but God will give us the grace as parents and can give our children the strength to not enter illicit sexual encounters. I remember watching recently a video-clip with the late Dr. Myles Munroe introducing his beloved wife of thirty-one years as the woman who "took my virginity when we got married". How many males could boast of practicing abstinence until marriage?

McGee gives further guidelines:

Teenagers benefit from conversations that identify the differences between love and lust and the self-esteem that comes from responsibly managing these feelings...Getting emotionally close to another person, taking the risk of telling someone our thoughts and feelings with the hope that the feelings will be returned—this can be enormously pleasurable and also frightening.

[http://www.advocatesforyouth.org/parents]

I was one of those teens who experienced "young love". I learnt from then, not to take for granted an adolescent's expressions of attraction and love for someone. There were of course many crushes (infatuations) in my early teen. At one stage, every few months there was another crush. However, there was one that lasted about a year. We entered a relationship and were emotionally attached but never sexually involved. This was the relationship which I revealed to my teacher. When that relationship broke up after a year, I was truly crushed! It took me several years to get over this particular person. He returned after about fourteen months and three broken relationships later, to renew the relationship. I made a decision that it would be unwise to, having noticed some serious behavioural changes in him and facing the fact that I myself had changed too (I had now become a

Christian). This decision was taken knowing that I was still "in love" with him.

When we met again years after, I realized I had not fully gotten over him. I had met several other guys – musician, pilot-in-training, other professionals but none grabbed my heart like my teenage lover. What am I saying? Young people can truly fall in love and we need to guide them into what to do and how to handle these deep emotions. Mrs. Vernon, my teacher, was the adult in my life at that time to give me guidance. Having found out that I had a boyfriend, she quickly encouraged me to reveal this to my mother and to let my Mom meet him, to use her words, "in case of anything". I guess she was being realistic recognizing that we are all prone to temptations. I did follow through.

These emotions in an adult can be tough to handle, even more so in a teen who fears rejection of his/her feelings by the other. That teen might need a shoulder to cry on when disappointments in "love relationships" come about. I have had to assist with counselling young people, especially males, who were almost losing it (displaying mental instability) when such a relationship came to an end. Parents need to be there to share their own experiences of winning and losing in the arena of love relationships and to encourage them. At that point, they don't usually want to hear that "there are more fish in the sea". They only know that their heart sees and went after that one "fish" that they don't want to lose! There is one final guideline by McGee that many parents struggle with at this stage. He writes:

> ... *we, as parents, should appreciate the fact that our teens will seem to be paying much more attention to their peers than to us. Nonetheless, we are critically important throughout this process, and we need to continue to be involved in our youngsters' lives. [http://www.advocatesforyouth.org/parents]*

As parents, we have to deal with what seems like rejection – our child is rejecting us and choosing their friends and peers over us. This is usually a temporary and transient state. If parents have had healthy and solid real-ationship with their children, the children soon grow out of this mental muddle and come back around to, after doing some mature analysis, conclude that their parents are important and that many of their principles are indeed correct. Rule of thumb: keep the real-ationship with the teen going, even when there is the feeling of "rejection" in the air.

Developing Healthy Relationships With The Opposite Sex

This should have been taught from the child was very young. However, this would be a good time to have mature talks with your young adult child to ensure that they have their heads "properly screwed on" to make healthy choices. These choices have to do with choosing the right person as a life-partner. As teenagers and young people, at a Christian retreat, we were asked to make a list of the top qualities that we believe our future mates should have. At that stage, we were forced to think it through. I had not had that

80

kind of exposure or teaching. In my home and within my neighbourhood, relationships that seemed healthy and stable were rare. There was much "shacking-up", even among the elderly. Marriage did not seem to be important. Even within those relationships, there was often physical and verbal abuse that the entire neighbourhood was aware of. My mother had kept herself celibate and was raising my youngest brother and myself, on her own.

The type of relationships that I saw did not impress me. It made me even question whether or not great men could be found. It was not until I began to meet and relate to Christian young and older men, and saw some of these men loving their wives that my perspective began to change. I had to try to do some learning about how to relate to the opposite sex in a healthy manner, by observation and much reading about relationships, especially how God intended man and woman to relate. It was unfortunate that while attempting to learn, I also had close interactions with males that behaved in an abusive manner. I had to keep my mind set on what God's ideal was for this type of intimate relationship. Some persons thought that I was being idealistic and setting my standards too high. This paid off in the end as I am now married to someone who truly depicts a godly man, and together we are able to work towards that ideal – a healthy relationship between a man and a woman. My teenage "list" is now complete. (smile)

Establishing Dating Guidelines

This has to do with appropriate age to date, individual versus group dating, acceptable behaviour while on a date, safe places to be on a date, etc. There is usually a tussle within homes around age-appropriateness for dating. Parents and children often differ in their views, and parents are often seen as the ones who are archaic in their beliefs. Parents don't always agree either on this topic. How do we decide appropriateness?

Firstly, a parent / guardian would need to ascertain if the child even understands what dating is. There is doting which speaks of fondness and infatuation, what we called in school, having a "crush" on someone, which might be the teacher standing before you who you did not speak to outside of the classroom. Dating then would be taking these feelings a step further. Dating is actually going out with that person. Spending a lot of time with him/her more than with other friends. If the going out is not double-dating, then there might not be anything to worry about. Groups of teens are known to hang out together at the mall; going to the movies but it is done as a group. Each might "like" a member of that group with a "special feeling" but that's as far as it goes. Yes, they might sit beside each other in class or at the movies. They might text or call each other but they are aware that they are too young for anything serious!

Serious dating however is another matter. How do we make this decision re when our child can start dating?

82

So when is a child ready for one-on-one dating? There's no right answer, even if most parents feel strongly that sometime around age 35 is perfect. It's important to consider your child as an individual. Consider their emotional maturity and sense of responsibility. For many kids, 16 seems to be an appropriate age, but it may be entirely suitable for a mature 15-year-old to go on a date, or to make your immature 16-year-old wait a year or two.

... When you've made a decision, be clear with your child about your expectations. Explain if and how you want your child to check in with you while they're out, what you consider acceptable and appropriate behavior, and curfew. [www.healthline.com]

Dating-age therefore I agree has more to do with maturity than biology. I would however suggest that it is better for our teens to go out with a mixed-gender group and learn how to relate to members of the opposite sex. It provides them an opportunity to get to know several males and to make comparisons in terms of qualities they would like in a life-partner when they are ready to settle down.

If your teen has a "crush" on someone that seems to be affecting them negatively then it's certainly time to sit and talk with them about it. If for example, he/she is isolating from the family and other friends; if their schoolwork and attendance is being affected; if there are serious mood swings and irritability, then you will need to step in. Your teen could be finding himself/herself in a place of compromising their standards. They could be dealing with being bullied into certain actions. They may be coerced into believing that this is the only relationship that matters and are manipulated into spending all of their time with that "friend". In instances where the child seems unreachable emotionally, the help of a school guidance-counsellor may have to be sought. Do whatever you need, but sensitively and with much wisdom, to rescue your teen from a possible bottomless emotional sinkhole.

What should be acceptable behaviour while on a date? How far should one go in terms of physical closeness and affection? Really, how far is too far?! Do you know that young people desire guidance – guidelines given in a loving and respectful manner? It is true that they don't always listen or want to follow but, there are many who don't want to mess up and to make irreversible mistakes. So if they know that you care and have their best interest at heart, they will listen.

I can recall seeing a young man in a church yard with a big hickey. I remarked with a smile: "Wow...looks like a big mosquito bit you." He quickly covered his neck and smiled sheepishly. I saw it as an opportunity to engage this young person who I had related to on different occasions, in a moment of truth. To find out what was happening just in case he was wading in waters too deep for him, we spoke and he did open up. I was able to guide him at the time. Thank God, he was able to correct some things that were going out of balance. He did not end up marrying that person but waited until he found who he wanted and needed.

Some young ladies have come and confided in me when they are feeling pressured in a relationship, internally or externally, to have sex. They wanted to rightly so, wait until marriage. I have been asked to intervene to speak to the male friend. This I had to do sensitively and respectfully so they would listen. Thank God that they did.

Many will listen if you are real with them. If you speak to them in the context of a real-ationship, being real with them about mistakes you have made in your own youth; how foolish you were at times; how strongly you felt perhaps at their age about someone; how far you went throwing caution to the wind, etc. I will never forget the words of a young man at an international intergenerational gathering. The session was about "passing a baton to the next generation(s)". The adults in the room were batting hard for releasing the young people to run the next leg; getting out of their way so they can have a chance to do it their way. A young man walked up to the mike and said, "While we are asking for independence and respect, we are not asking to be left alone. We cannot do this alone. We still need you." Those words hit me so hard and registered to me that there is no stepping away from them to let them conquer the world. We do need to loosen our grip as they are getting older and make room for their growth but never to abandon our roles as mentors, counsellors, advisors, tutors, coaches and consultants.

Appropriate Dating Behaviour:

This has a lot to do with **what the individual can handle without it becoming stimulating towards building a desire for sexual expression.** Humans are all different and what is a stimulant to one might not in the least be stimulating to another. For one person, even a peck on the lips is a turn on. For such a person then, a peck on the lips is too far. For one person, someone touching their hair could be very stimulating while for another, it might be like touching their fingernail. No feeling. We then need to teach our teens to be aware of their bodies and what sensations they have when listening to certain music and conversations. They need to be aware of how they feel when someone they might be fond of is sitting very close to them or there is skin-touching-skin. We are not sending them out to do experiments to find out. What we are helping them with is awareness.

A friend of mine was standing beside me at church. A brother came up and hugged her from behind with his head near her neck. She jumped and when I looked at her, she was flushed from head-to-toe. She quickly exclaimed: "Don't ever do that again!" Afterwards she told me that her neck area is her "weak spot". She stays clear of hugging in that area. For an ex-boyfriend of mine, a similar thing happened. His was being hugged from behind. He warned me not to ever do that! I respected his boundaries. Both
86

these persons were aware that they had "trigger spots" that could get them in trouble and warned others of respecting these boundaries. Our children need to be taught to do that and not to be afraid of others' reactions when they do so.

Both of the parties should be committed to setting limits in the relationship and keeping these boundaries. We who have passed through dating and courtship know that this is not an easy task. Sometimes passion flares. However, many individuals have made it into a marriage without having sexual intercourse, or even petting because they both had the same convictions about how far not to go before marriage. When it becomes painfully difficult is when one or both parties have no boundaries. They want the whole pie even if there is no solid commitment. They want their sexual gratification and if they don't get it, they break up and move on to where they can get it. Some don't even wait to bring closure but cheat in what should be an exclusive relationship. About a month before marriage, I had to request very little physical contact to be made between my fiancé and myself since things were mounting and a "horse" within me was getting ready to burst the gates! I could not afford for us, having kept ourselves to that point to do anything foolish. Thank God that my fiancé respected my wishes. This was made easier since he too was committed to celibacy.

(c) **Know the difference between love and lust!** Lust cannot wait! It cannot wait to get physical! Lust cannot wait to see the relationship set straight by a timely consideration of a marital commitment, which sets the couple on a path of being real with each other in every area. Even if this relationship is moving towards the serious commitment of marriage, there needs to be consistent self-control exercised, because lust cannot be satisfied to stay within boundaries. It is always pressing beyond the confines of the stages or type of relationship. It seeks to cross a threshold that has dire consequences that are not usually seen at the moment, when one is blinded by the craving for pleasure. However, when one gives in and the pleasure is over and reality sets in, there is usually shame and regret that you have breached your standards.

Lust is a strong craving or a strong desire for something. It is frequently used in the context of sex, but it can be anything. Usually, there is a deception when lust is allowed to unleash itself. The individual usually thinks that he/she has absolutely no control – they have to do what they are craving to do. They flirt and allow themselves to be tempted. It's sort of placing one's hand at the mouth of the lion, daring him to bite it. Not realizing that you may not be as strong as you think you are, to flee the temptation as it presents itself. Sometimes sense and sensibility; even caution is thrown to the wind so there is a feeling that only this moment of pleasure matters and all will be well! Although we may know the truth from knowledge on the subject or from hearing past experiences, we can fool ourselves into thinking, "This won't happen to me!"

(d) **There are more critical qualities to build in the relationship long before it should get to the stage of sexual expression**. In Jamaica, Dr. Barry Davidson, counselling psychologist and CEO of Family Life Ministries, wrote **"Before you say I do"** a premarital counseling questionnaire and manual. (1991). Some of his views were expressed in an article in the Jamaica Observer, March 05, 2012:

> *"You have to really seriously do premarital counselling, because people can deceive you and you get married and find yourself dealing with something you never bargained for," said the psychologist who has been doing marriage, family and individual counselling since 1981...*
>
> *"Once you seem to be interested in somebody, and you are thinking marriage, you should do premarital counselling," said Dr. Davidson, who pointed out that about 40 per cent of those who come in for premarital counselling usually decide to call off the wedding because of the information gleaned about their partner during the sessions*
>
> [http://www.jamaicaobserver.com, NADINE WILSON, Monday, March 05, 2012]

As a counsellor, having had Dr. Davidson as a lecturer at Graduate School and through my years of counselling, I am sold out on this conviction. It has also been my experience that many couples, regardless of their age, have postponed engagement, a wedding and have even decided to break an engagement because they were now facing up to some facts. They had to face the fact that they were discovering some things within themselves or their partner, that if they found that out while in a marriage, it would be next to impossible to build a strong marriage. At that stage there might be regret and deep disappointment. Even if there is pregnancy, we discourage marriage, until premarital counselling is done, since pregnancy is not a good reason to get married.

What is even sadder is that often dating relationships have rushed to the ultimate sexual expressions without even the talk of the future, commitment, the meeting of family members and the prospect of marriage. This is not a real-ationship if the two don't know each other intimately on other levels. It is after emotional, social, spiritual, intellectual and creative intimacy is achieved and the couple is satisfied with the real-ationship, that the culminating of this intimacy into sexual intimacy should take place in the context of marriage. What's the point of having great sex but want to kill each other afterwards!

There are two words that every teen should learn to embrace so that even when parents and others aren't around, you can grab hold of them. They are, **Wisdom** which comes from God and, **Vision** which has to do with having insight into where you want to go, and the things that will help you to get there. It is really finding out your divine purpose. Why were you created? Wisdom has to do with how we skillfully apply the knowledge we have, using discretion and discernment. The book of Proverbs in the

Bible was written by the wisest man that ever lived, King Solomon. Just the study of this book will give us guidelines of how we can escape evil and avoid bringing our lives to ruins. Above that, it sheds the light on how to build good real-ationships.

The next chapter will take us into the rudiments of real-ationships within a marriage.

Image by SaadiaAMYii from Pixabay

CHAPTER THREE

BONDED: THIS IS FOR LIFE

> *"The real act of marriage takes place in the heart, not in the ballroom or church or synagogue. It's a choice you make - not just on your wedding day, but over and over again - and that choice is reflected in the way you treat your husband or wife-- Barbara De Angelis*

When some persons hear that they are going to be bonded for life if they should get married, they panic, want to run away, wonder if they can manage better with a single life, have a flood of memories of failed relationships, whether theirs or others. Some would even go as far as to discourage others; what the bible terms as "forbidding to marry". We do need to unequivocally affirm that marriage is of God and was ordained by God. It is God's ideal for sexual intimacy between a male and a female, in addition to meeting other needs such as companionship and procreation. Marriage, therefore, has to come with deep commitment of each party in order to get the greatest fulfillment of what God intended marriage to be.

While doing my post-graduate studies, one lecturer pointed out from a research done that there were five top reasons for divorce.

- Communication

- Finance

- Sex

- Religion

- In-laws

This was in the late 80s. Currently the list includes: *Adultery, Addiction and Lack of Support in Good Times, Incompatibility with Finances* [*http://www.divorcemag.com*]. Added to some already listed, another website named, *Constant Arguing, Weight Gain, Unrealistic Expectations, Lack of Intimacy, Lack of Equality, Not Being Prepared for Marriage, and Abuse* [*https://www.marriage.com*] As we look at the primary reasons given for why people say they get divorced, these reasons point to where the emphasis then should be when a man and woman are considering 'tying the knot' and for sure, where pre-marital counsellors have to do their thorough investigating when counselling the couple for marriage. Dr. Barry Davidson, a founding Director and CEO of Family Life Ministries in Jamaica, has written a book, "*Before They Say I Do*", which is a very well put together manual for pre-marital counsellors and couples preparing for marriage.

94

Dr. Gary Chapman, in "A Love Language Minute" focused his readers' attention on the topic of "Why Get Married". In Part 2, having discussed seven common purposes of marriage, he pointed us to the **deepest purpose** of marriage in an adaptation from his own book, "The Five Love Languages Singles Edition":

> *"In the ancient biblical account of Creation, God says of Adam, "It is not good for the man to be alone." God's answer to man's need was "I will make a helper suitable for him." The Hebrew word for suitable literally means "face-to-face." The picture is that God created one with whom man could have a face-to-face relationship. It speaks of that kind of in-depth, personal relationship whereby the two are united in an unbreakable union that satisfies the deepest longings of the human heart.*
>
> *Marriage is God's answer for humanity's deepest need-union of life with another. Indeed, that same ancient account of creation says of Adam and Eve, "They will become one flesh." [Adapted from: **The Five Love Languages Singles Edition]***

Dr. Gary Chapman is well respected for his study on relationships and especially on helping marriage partners to discover what it is that makes their beloved spouse tick. Chapman addresses man's desire for connection with another human being. I will be examining some of his pointers in his narrative to singles in which he teaches them some truths about marriage. The bottom line for me is how we can make marriage real, the way God intended it to be. I believe it starts in the mind with having a clear understanding of what marriage is; from whom this concept came about; from where we can find some guidelines for meandering this somewhat difficult pathway of understanding someone on an intimate level and making such a union real. Chapman writes,

> *"I believe that marriage is designed to be the most intimate of all human relationships... they are going to share life to such a degree that they become "one flesh." This does not mean that married couples lose their individuality, but it does mean that they have a deep sense of unity." [The Five Love Languages Singles Edition]*

There is no closer human relationship than the one between a husband and wife. There is no other relationship that makes the two become ONE. A kind of bond that makes whatever the other do, even with his/her own body affects the other to the core. Marriage is built by God to meet human beings deepest need for intimacy on the human level. I say on the human level because there is a level of intimacy that we need spiritually that only God can fulfill. This is divine intimacy. The problem sometimes is that we try to use people to fulfill our need for divine intimacy and sometimes, even in marriage, "crucify" the spouse if they cannot!

God has reserved this area of intimacy for Himself! However, in the marriage union, the one-flesh experience can also be a spiritual experience of the two in such union with God and sharing that union with each other, that spiritually they are walking in agreement and unity. This is real and not a figment of the imagination. Couples who have experienced this unity can report a greater sense of fulfillment in their marriage than those who have not encountered this level. It is interesting that one of the ten top reasons for divorce reported, is religious differences [https://stearns-law.com/blog/divorce/the-top-10-reasons-marriages-end-in-divorce]. Religion, if seen as merely a practice of rituals and strict adherence to a set of rules, can separate even the couples that were so "in love with each other" if they strongly disagree with each other in this area. However, a right relationship with God, where He is allowed first place in that union and we are submitted to His guidance and wisdom in each of our lives and within the space of that marriage, can bring an unbelievable peace and fulfillment that is better felt than told.

Chapman points out a couple things that will be examined here to assist you in determining whether or not you had the right perspective when you entered marriage and if changing your perspective on the reason for such a union as marriage, will also bring the kind of transformation in your marriage that you have longed for:

What Marriage is NOT: [Adapted from The Five Love Languages Singles Edition]

"Marriage is not a contract to make sexual relationships legal." - Chapman

The people outside of a context where there is a strong Scriptural conviction, for example in Christianity, that sex outside of marriage is not only wrong but an abomination before God, may easily end up making the mistake of getting married to legalize sex. After all, their bodies are crying out for sexual fulfillment but they don't want to displease God. Sexual fulfillment, on its own, cannot be a primary reason for marriage. If it is then at times when that fulfillment is not available to the couple, e.g. during times of illness, geographical separation for extended periods, times of sexual dysfunctions, etc. what would be the glue to keep that marriage together if the reason why they are really together is gone? Those who have entered marriage with this as their primary reason has had the rude awakening that sex is not always glitters and fireworks. There can be disappointments, down days, dysfunctional moments, depressive episodes, derailment of plans, and death of desires. **Sex** has also been given as one of the top reasons for divorce: ***Your spouse doesn't understand / fulfill your needs and desires***. [https://stearns-law.com/blog/divorce/the-top-10-reasons-marriages-end-in-divorce]   Some persons might quickly want to quote from 1 Cor 7:36 – " If anyone is worried that he might not be acting honorably toward the virgin he is engaged to, and it his passions are too strong and he feels he ought to marry, he should do as he wants. He is not sinning. They should get married."   In this context, he has been in a relationship with the female. They have been building an intimate relationship on other levels and in other areas. They seem now to be at the place where their bodies are crying out for the next level of fulfillment and the encouragement being given is, get married.

I do want to encourage especially my Christian readers and others who desire to walk according to their convictions of celibacy that you do not enter into marriage to "legalize sex". If self-control is the issue then God is able to help you to cultivate that fruit in your life which will greatly benefit you when you do get married. There is excessive stimulation visually and otherwise around us, especially with the onset of technology and quick access to all forms of the media. However, you cannot afford to allow this constant stimulation to push you into the serious commitment of marriage, if other areas are not intact for the call to such a mature union, nor into an illicit sexual relationship in order to fulfill those desires. Though each decision might bring instant pleasure, the long-term effects and consequences are too costly and painful to choose either of these roads. If marriage is the answer to lack of self-control, when you now have all the sex you can get within the marriage, why are some still looking outside of the marriage for more fulfillment?

"It is not merely a social institution to provide for the care of children." - Chapman

I can hear my male readers with a resounding "Yes" to this point that Chapman makes. Reason being, this is usually the female partner's mistake. It is true that marriage is the right and ideal context for children to be raised. Relating to a mother and father who are firstly a part of a committed relationship with each other. This does give the children a strong sense of security. However, the mistake made, especially by females is to see this as the ultimate reason for the union and after child-bearing, to minimize the ongoing need for fulfillment of their partner's needs. There is a strong sense of fulfillment that comes with having children in the home, however, this fulfillment cannot and should not replace the conscious working at fulfilling your partner's emotional and physical needs, which do not go away with the fulfillment of other needs, example of child-rearing. Research has actually shown that the marital relationship often declines with the entrance of children into the union, and many avoid divorce for the sole reason of staying together to raise these children.

> *For around 30 years, researchers have studied how having children affects a marriage, and the results are conclusive: the relationship between spouses suffers once kids come along. Comparing couples with and without children, researchers found that the rate of the decline in relationship satisfaction is nearly twice as steep for couples who have children than for childless couples. In the event that a pregnancy is unplanned, the parents experience even greater negative impacts on their relationship.[fortune.com]*

I can recall sitting in the pediatrician's office when my son was a year old. She looked at my husband and I and asked, "What is he still doing sleeping in your bedroom?" Now, he was not sleeping on our bed but in his crib, which was inside our bedroom. I am sure my eyes did not hide the surprise at such a question. After all, he is only a year old! So I thought, but I understood what she was suggesting. She was indicating that we both, as a couple, need to get back to the freedom of being a couple in our matrimonial space without having to consider the presence of a now growing child.

We decided to take her advice and fixed up his room. I prayed for God's guidance on the matter as I was anticipating him being resistant and not wanting to be alone in a room. I remember painting cartoon figures on his closet. Using stencils to paint different figures on the walls and generally doing stuff to make his room "child-friendly". I then began to announce with great excitement, in his presence, when we had visitors, "This is DeMario's room!" They would clap their hands with exhilaration repeating what I said. He enjoyed the moment and soon began to show the room by himself. We had no problem getting him to sleep by himself in his own room after this. Phew! We had to face a fear and get past it and so will many parents, especially mothers.

I have met persons who have said to me, I cannot get him/her out of my bed! These children were up to eight years old! The first question that entered my mind was, how is this marriage functioning, especially re intimacy in all areas. When and where do they speak privately? Where do they go for physical intimacy? Some may say, in the child's room. However, this is not appropriate boundary-setting. Children should be taught to appreciate that their parents have a space that they can only visit from time-to-time. The door should be knocked on to gain permission for entry and when it is bedtime, they head to their own room. This is having a proper real-ationship with our children since in the larger world, they will have to respect other people's boundaries and they learn this at home.

In an article, "*What Kids Learn from Your Marriage*", the fact is made very clearly that parents model for children what they should be and become in their adult years.

> *Turns out there is copious research to suggest that modeling—a fancy word for behaving in a way you want others to replicate—is a key but often overlooked component in a child's development. "Modeling takes place even before kids can understand verbal communication," explains Elizabeth R. Lombardo, Ph.D., a psychologist in Wexford, Pennsylvania...As parents, we so often focus on teaching verbally, but we forget the importance of our actions." And no interactions are more visible—or powerful—to a child than what transpires between Mom and Dad. It's not just division of labor or gender-role stuff that matters; a longitudinal study published in 2009 by the U.S. Department of Health and Human Services found that the quality of a child's parents' marriage had as much influence on his or her future mental and physical health and well-being as his or her own relationship with either parent.*
>
> *[www.parents.com/parenting/better-parenting/advice/what-kids-learn-from-your-marriage/]*

So, the facts are, if parents choose to view and use their marriage as only a "social institution" for their children, not only will that marriage suffer but wrong seeds are being sown in the minds of their children, for how marriage ought to be and how parents should relate in a healthy manner when children come along.

"It is not merely a psychological clinic where we gain the emotional support we need." - Chapman

The operative word here for me is "gain". Another term I would use is "seeking to get". One of the things I have learned in real-ationships and especially in the context of marriage is that it is more about giving than getting! The truth is, if both partners are willing to focus on giving; on meeting the needs of the other then ultimately both will gain from the relationship. I think what often goes wrong here is that marriage is entered with the focus on what we can get; when we can get it - which is every time we want it; how we can get it, oftentimes with the use of manipulation and intimidation.

Many arguments and fights in marriage are around this – I am not getting what I "want" from you! Sometimes each person is shouting the same sentiments at the other but no one is listening to say "well, if I do my part and my partner does his/her part, both our needs would be met." The gaining of social support then should come from each person's decision that he/she wants to give that kind of support to their partner. It cannot be demanded, grabbed, coerced or extracted through intimidation. If done so, then it is not truly support. In a marriage real-ationship, support should be voluntary and lovingly offered for the maximum benefit to the other.

"It is not a means of gaining social status or economic security." - Chapman

How many times have we heard of persons feeling "used" in a marriage when they realize that the ultimate reason for being chosen was to be seen as a status symbol. As a result, they fall in line with the other status symbols – a certain type of house, car, job, and neighbourhood. The person doing the choosing, depending on which social group he/she might want to fit in might choose to marry someone based on their education, family of origin, job status, financial strength, accomplishments in the marketplace, Christian ministry, popularity, power base. Whatever the category, it is wrong and it is unfair to the partner who is now that "symbol". The "symbol" goes through a marriage knowing that he/she was not chosen because of who they are – their personality, character. The main attraction was a selfish one. It was about what the other party could get out of them especially while profiling with them.

Women tend to fall into the trap of marrying primarily for social and/or financial security. Especially those living in Third World countries and poor nations, the temptation is always there to marry, not out of love but convenience. If the person can provide for them a house, perhaps a car and meet other material needs, then he becomes a prime target. Various expressions have been used to describe the provider – "Santa", "Boops", and "Sugar Daddy".

What tends to happen to the perpetrator is that he/she, not marrying for the right reasons, when they meet someone who they are truly attracted to and with whom they may even have "fallen-in-love", the marriage partner gets hell!

The Issue of Rebound

Have you ever seen someone who was in an obviously deep romantic relationship with another then they broke up, only days after or perhaps a few weeks/ months, they are back into another serious relationship and may even be talking about getting married. If there was not a "love-triangle" prior to the break up then there is rebound involved. What is rebound?

*A person might be considered on the **rebound** if he or she becomes involved in a **relationship** that shortly follows the ending of a previous one. ... If you are dating someone who is **rebounding**, you may wonder if he or she is capable of* *emotional attachment or if you are, instead, simply a substitute for love that was lost.*

["Rebound" Relationships | Psychology Today - https://www.psychologytoday.com.]

Having experienced a rebound relationship myself, I can confirm that it is a very painful situation, not only for the person who is the "victim" but for the one who wakes up to discover that they are not truly attracted to the person in the current relationship, but is still "in love" with the previous person. That's a wake-up-call that is not easy to deal with especially when you are committed to having real-ationhips, but don't want to hurt this current person. I was the one who had the wake-up-call. As a young adult, I was seated at a wedding and watching my friend, dressed in a dashing-outfit and emceeing with such eloquence. As I watched, I felt myself becoming emotionally distant then comparing him with the previous boyfriend. It was scary. This went on for the entire reception and when it was time to go, I wanted to leave alone – not with him. Even scarier to me was the fact that he insisted on taking me home. I could not hide my feelings. We had an open real-ationship. I was not sure of the reasons, having not done deep analysis as yet, but I just knew I could not go on. He did not have my heart!

I requested that night, a break in our relationship – some time for me to think. The disappointment was obvious, but the meltdown did not come until we were at Church the following morning. He broke down in front of the congregation. I was in deep conflict but moved towards him and stood with him. I felt like a worm knowing fully well what had caused this, but I could not play the hypocrite. He was a good guy and deserved to have someone who truly loved him for who he is. We never got back together. A few years later, I was a guest at his wedding, joyful that he had found true love. Persons who had negative things to say before were now thanking me for being honest with him and felt that the experience we had was not all negative. As a matter of fact, it was he who said, as we spoke after the Church-incident, that we can take away the "rose" from what we had together rather than focus on the thorns. I chose to take the rose and I think so did he.

Of course, I had work to do. After that break-up, I had to deal with my own heart. I had to cut soul-ties to this previous "love" who was now married to our mutual friend! It took a while but finally I was free, and could now move on to give my heart again. Before marriage or even committing ourselves in a romantic relationship, we should properly examine whether we had fully dealt with any previous relationships – hurts, disappointments, rejection, abuses.

Chapman writes:

The ultimate purpose of marriage is not even achieved when it is the vehicle for love and companionship, as valuable as these are.

The supreme purpose of marriage is the union of a man and woman at the deepest possible level and in all areas of life, which in turn brings the greatest possible sense of fulfillment to the couple and best serves the purposes of God for their lives. [What Marriage is NOT: [Adapted from The Five Love Languages Singles Edition]

Is a Divorce Inevitable?

Walking through a divorce is no "stroll in the park". Some persons who got married never envisioned themselves having ever to face such a traumatic experience. Even if the marriage was "hell on earth", divorce is still a painful affair. Whatever the reason, divorce can be traumatic and for those of us who have walked through it, it feels like death! It is no wonder that the Bible says that God hates it.

Apart from the pain of separation between the couple going through the divorce, the judgmental attitudes that follow; the gossip that is aroused; the splitting of the family when children are involved; the decisions re the dividing of the assets achieved together; the reaction of family members, friends and organization members and partners are enough to send the two parties over the deep end emotionally. The type of sensitivity to the couple that is needed at this time is not often meted out. The blame-game begins sometimes with their own children and relatives. How does one return to being "single" (although, this not the legal term for a divorced person)? It almost seems more costly to divorce than to stay together in some cases. However, we do live in a real world and there are legitimate reasons and circumstances that may ultimately lead to a divorce – the final and legal dissolution of a marriage. One of the things I have learnt to respect is how different persons are in coping with various stressors in our lives. What builds someone through trials might break someone else, even beyond repair. In Jamaica, we have some sayings: "What is joke to you is death to me" and "What is one man's meat, is another's poison". This is just a reminder to us that people are affected differently by the same circumstances.

What Often Causes Divorce?

Before listing some of the reasons for divorce, I would hasten to say that the inevitability of divorce might have been set before the marriage took place! A bold statement I know, but there are some obvious red flags and flashing amber lights before a marriage takes place that we choose to ignore. When these are ignored, the marriage most likely would be starting on shaky foundation. It usually takes a miracle; much counselling; a deep resolve in the hearts of **both** individuals and the grace of God to make this marriage work. What are some general reasons given for divorce?

1. **Hardening of The Heart**: The best place to start is what the Bible states as the primary and underlying cause for divorce.

Jesus referred to it as "hardness of heart". Matthew 19:8-9 (MSG) states it like this:

> *Jesus said, "Moses provided for divorce as a concession to your hard heartedness, but it is not part of God's original plan. I'm holding you to the original plan, and holding you liable for adultery if you divorce your faithful wife and then marry someone else. I make an exception in cases where the spouse has committed adultery."*

Jesus makes it very plain that whatever reasons we give, apart from his exceptional cause(s), one or both persons has to harden his/her own heart. It seems to me that whatever the difficulties, if the heart of each is humble and open to correction, and the receiving of help and serious intervention (divine and human), there will always be a chance for proper reconciliation.

What then is "hardness of heart"? I believe it is coming to a place where the mind makes a decision to shut itself off from responding to another person; the emotions follow and gets to a neutral, if not a negative place when it comes to any feeling of sentiments where the other party is concerned; an unwillingness to have compassion when the he/she is obviously suffering; losing every desire to be near the other party, whether emotionally or physically. Usually this person is self-driven and "doing me", not caring about the effect on especially his/her spouse. Oftentimes it is accompanied by ignorance and a "darkness in understanding" of what is happening to the other party and within the marital relationship. A person does not have to be a Christian to experience and identify with this reality of the hardening of one's heart. All types of abuse have this characteristic buried somewhere in the perpetrator's heart.

God has to be brought into the picture in such a person's mind, and to an extent that the individual is broken and contrite. Since pride and arrogance often accompany the hardness of heart, then the opposite features of **humility** will be required, something that is hard to achieve when one is holding on to their rights, and believing in the situation of a broken marriage that they are right. It is a self-righteousness that takes hold of the individual that blinds him/her to truth about self; truth about God; truth about one's mate, etc. So this humility is a "letting-go-and-allowing-God" to fix only what He can fix. Allowing Him to get you the right help that you need. It is a taking "human hands off" the relationship and allowing God who alone knows all of men's hearts, to fix it. When He is given a free hand, it is marvelous what He can do! God will invest Himself in helping the couple to fix it. Reason. God hates divorce.

Emotional Immaturity of One or Both Parties. Having dealt with the cause for divorce, in my own experience, especially in the counselling room, I would rank this as a top reason. I know that no one enters a marriage and has the areas of Communication, Finance, Sex, Religion, In-laws, etc., perfectly sorted out. The trouble comes many times with an emotional immaturity that perpetuates an inability to tackle problems in a realistic manner when issues surrounding these areas arise. As the couple are building real-ationship and "rubber-meets-the-road"; they now hit a "pothole", and it is the way that each party approaches the problem that will make a super difference.

What is emotional immaturity? In an article entitled,

5 Signs You're Dating An Emotionally Immature Partner

(August 31, 2017) **Samantha Burns, a Relationship Counselor** writes:

> *Emotional immaturity can reflect a lack of depth and understanding about one's own emotions, inability to communicate and process things related to the relationship, as well as lack of empathy and ability to understand your partner's emotional experiences.*

> *Having an emotionally immature partner can impact the overall health of your relationship. Often times these partners have a "me" factor over a "we" factor, so they can come off as selfish or unable to take your feelings into account.*

> *When there's conflict, an emotionally immature partner may blame you, rather than be able to process how his or her actions contributed to the issue.*

> *It may be difficult to have calm, effective communication when talking about anything of substance. There could be deflection through humor, or just an avoidance of emotionally intimate conversations.*

> *[https://bossedup.org/5-signs-youre-dating-an-emotionally-immature-partner/]*

Although I have often said, "Marriage is not pickney business", translated, "Marriage is NOT for children", I do not refer here to biological age. Pickney and children are both used to describe not chronological age but the qualities of a child that are often found in persons that can be mature in age but immature in disposition. It's, for example, a forty-year-old behaving like a sixteen year-old! Children truly cannot enter into marriage because they are not ready, even if their bodies and hormones tell them otherwise. They are not ready to enter into the serious commitment and sacrifice that come with the terrain of marriage.

The emotionally immature spouse will be wanting his/her way; throwing temper-tantrums or even being verbally and physically abusive if they don't get their way; mashing up furniture and other articles if they are mad with their partner, children, others; wanting to drive their vehicle over a cliff because they don't feel they can control their spouse; will not truly allow others to intervene to help them; will want you exclusively, and rant and rave if you have friends who care about you; will do whatever they can, in their power to separate and isolate their partner from his/her family and friends.

If you are in such a relationship and you are discussing marriage, you are not ready, whether it is you or your partner that fits this profile. To enter into a marriage without you or the other party fixing themselves, is courting disaster! Apart from premarital counselling, the immature party needs to get personal

114

counselling to deal with the "baggage" he/she is often carrying from their past. I heard it once said, "The past is not passed unless properly processed". That disturbing past will turn up in your present marriage and create such a tempestuous marriage that your future only looks like hurricanes coming over the horizon. There will hardly be times of peace. If it is you, get help now and if it is someone you care about, encourage him/her to get help.

A Lack of Communication Skills. Sometimes in premarital or marital counselling, the counsellor has to take the client(s) back to basics in the proper way to communicate with their loved one. Surveys done on What Breaks up Marriages and Qualities of Healthy Marriages, show Communication at the top of those lists. Therefore, communication is a top reason for marital breakup and a top reason given for marital success.

> *A new survey confirms what your premarital counselor knew all along: the trick to staving off divorce lies in how effectively you and your spouse communicate.*
>
> *Lifestyle website YourTango.com polled 100 mental health professionals and found that communication problems was cited as the most common factor that leads to divorce (65 percent), followed by couples' inability to resolve conflict (43 percent).*
>
> *The survey also found that men and women have different communication complaints. Seventy percent of the experts surveyed said that men cite nagging and complaining as the top communication problem in their marriage. Women's top*

complaint was that their spouse doesn't validate their opinions or feelings enough, according to 83 percent of experts. [https://www.huffingtonpost.com/2013/11/20/divorce-causes]

Another survey, **Root Causes of Divorce** lie in poor communication, survey finds:

Poor communication between husbands and wives is the most common cause of divorce among Emiratis, according a new survey commissioned by the UAE Marriage Fund. The survey of 1,335 divorced Emirati men and women, carried out by a team of experts from UAE University, found that misunderstandings between spouses was most often cited as the cause of divorce,...

[https://www.thenational.ae/uae/root-causes-of-divorce-lie-in-poor-communication-survey]

By communication, we are referring to how each transfers information to the other, verbally or non-verbally, which would either allow the other to feel uplifted, encouraged, affirmed and more like royalty. On the other hand, each could speak to the other in berating, insulting, accusatory, a rude manner allowing the other to feel like a worm. The former lends to healthy real-ationships. Even when there is disagreement, each one needs to know how to speak to the other so there is a win-win approach to the relationship and they both learn something and benefit in a positive way from this conflict.

However, when the latter approach is taken, and a dangerous threshold is crossed; when derogatory words are used that have an imprint on the soul and can never really be recalled or its deathly effect reversed; when words are used that dig a grave for the relationship then communication is used negatively, and instead of building the other person, it breaks down the secure walls of intimacy, and disrupts any firm foundation that this marriage was built on. We all know those stinging words said in anger and resentment. Sadly to say, these words are sometimes used "in the name of the Lord" – the use of Bible verses to bash one's partner and the revealing of confidential information, instead of attempting to "cover" one's spouse as in the case of the biblical account of Joseph who out of love, when he thought Mary had been immoral, wanted to deal with the situation privately. Can you imagine what ,would have happened if Joseph went around telling others that Mary had slept with and gotten pregnant by another man? How would he reverse the damage of already sowing in people's minds through his communication that Mary was immoral? Even if he went around attempting to change that information and to convince people of the truth, people are people, and some would rather to believe the worst about others. The damage to the spouse's character cannot be totally reversed.

There are persons in marriages right now who are reeling from the unwise words of a spouse. The boisterous outbursts that bring the neighbours right into their bedroom. The neighbours don't need to turn down their devices to hear. It is loud enough for all those in ¼ mile radius to know that you are upset with your spouse and all the reasons why you are upset. The shame and embarrassment that often follows as the abused spouse and the children have to walk through that neighbourhood, knowing that they are being criticized, gossiped about or pitied. Hopefully some are being prayed for.

Some persons are misled into thinking that they are just speaking their minds and being real – that theirs is a real-ationship. A true real-ationship builds up. It does not dump all of its garbage on the other in the name of honesty, watching the other crumble psychologically and otherwise then step away feeling like mission accomplished. That approach is not a reflection of the type of love that partners should have, and have usually vowed to have for each other. That type of respect that makes you never want to cross a certain threshold no matter how angry and upset one becomes.

We must be our "brothers-keeper" and that should begin with our spouse. I remember my Mom used to say to one of my brothers who was abusive towards me, "If you say these things to your sister and call her these nasty names, how do you expect others outside to do differently? She had a point. A point that those prone to negative communication within their marriage should seriously think about.

What is Positive Communication to Build Healthy Marriages?

I don't know of anyone who goes into a marriage for it to fail. Do you? Therefore, since we all want successful marriages, we need to study the things that lend to us meeting such a goal. Positive communication is definitely one. Let's look at a few helpful tips as communication is in itself a large topic to cover, and an entire book could be devoted to cover it.

- ✓ **Recognize that there is a THRESHOLD NEVER TO CROSS**! The book of Proverbs reveals to us that the heart of the righteous weighs its answers (Prov. 15: 1-4,7, 28)

- ✓ **Not losing common courtesies** – maintaining a high level of respect for your partner. Saying 'Good morning'; 'Thank you'; 'Please', 'I am sorry', etc. are not words that should be left out of a marriage. These common courtesies do enhance a real-ationship and help each to feel validated and respected by the other. In other words, it ensures that we don't take our spouses for granted and lose respect for them. We honour them with our words and mannerisms.

- ✓ When there is disagreement and conflicts, it is, **knowing how to "fight" in a way that each can look justly at the situation and make a fair assessment** of each person's role in the conflict. This can be done without any type of abuse coming into play. As a matter of fact, if the issue can be placed as it were on the table and each looks at it, not being historical or hysterical, but maturely analyzing the problem, even if it cannot be resolved in one sit-down session, as both seek to forgive and work at a resolution, the real-ationship can continue to be rebuilt and reaffirmed.

✓ **Refusing to withdraw to the extent of building emotional walls** that the other cannot climb over. Ouch! This was one area that my husband and I had to watch out for and still have to be guarding against. We are both peace-loving and sometimes in order not to prolong a disagreement, we would both get quiet and hibernate into our own psychological caves. However, we soon learnt that this was hurting the other, so with much fighting that internal struggle for self-preservation, much self-control and definitely the help of the Lord, we have decided not to go there. So we have to talk it out, no matter how painful until we come to some agreeable resolution. Love grows even more at times when we come through an emotional storm together, each shielding the other from splinters that could fly and hurt the beloved partner

✓ **Meeting the other's need for positive communication.** There are some individuals who will not feel fulfilled in the relationship if they cannot have meaningful conversation with their own spouse. They need that sit-down time to talk about the day and its challenges and successes; some new challenges surmounted and conquered. If you don't care to listen, usually they will find someone, usually some friend on social media to listen. Gary Chapman puts it this way:

> *"Your emotional love language and the language of your spouse may be as different as Chinese from English. No matter how hard you try to express love in "English", if your spouse understands only "Chinese", you will never understand how to love each other.*
>
> *Being sincere is not enough. We must be willing to learn our spouse's primary love language if we are to be effective communicators of love."*
>
> *[https://www.focusonthefamily.com/marriage/communication-and-conflict]*

So, my husband has studied mine and knows that I need quality time – especially when going to bed, talking about the day is very relaxing for me and I make a deep connection with him when we can talk. I also know that he enjoys having little things done for him. I try, even when I am tired, to look out for these little things to do. I find that we have a fulfilling marriage because we focus on meeting each other's need for positive communication in the way that is meaningful to the other. I have discovered one truth. It is truly in sincerely giving that each one receives.

✓ **Having a Sense of Humor.** This goes a far way when you can laugh with each other. Laugh at yourself and your own mistakes. Laugh at each other's jokes and silly moments. Simply smiling with each other helps to make the other feel warm and positive in a world that is often cold and callous. If those outside of the home are demanding a particular image in the workplace, etc. isn't it great to know that you can "let your hair down" and have a liberating real-ationship with your spouse. Sometimes we sit together and are checking our messages. When a humourous one comes up, we share it and have a good laugh together. This lightens the atmosphere and balances it when you have to be talking about paying bills, unfair treatment from others, those who are sick, and about things that you cannot otherwise smile about.

What If My Spouse Doesn't Communicate?

My first answer to that is that we are always communicating. We only use different methods to do so. Even in our silence, we are communicating. When this problem turns up in the counselling room, I usually ask if this was always so – a non-communicative partner. The answer is usually "No". The next step then is to find out what has "shut down" this partner and their desire to communicate in the marriage. These are some of the reasons we have discovered.

- **Men and women communicate differently**. It is critical to understand this difference, so you won't be frustrated with each other. A female could tell her female friend to go do something for her and she moves and does it. No offense. Usually if the same is done to the male, he takes offense to you "commanding" him to do something/telling him what to do or even being disrespectful. This works vice-versa too, as buddies can talk rough to each other but if the same talk is taken home, a wife would be sensitive to this and see it even as you speaking in a thoughtless manner to her.

- **Men and women are sensitive in their own way**. We have heard about the "male ego" and how women react especially around the time of menstruation. Both species are sensitive. We therefore have to learn not to take things so personally. I had to learn this very early in marriage when my spouse was withholding an answer to a question I was asking. Upon further discussion, he revealed that he did not want to deal with a reaction! I had to pause and think about it. If I wanted him to feel free to speak with me about anything at all, I had to temper my reaction. It worked and is still working! I got the message: Men will shut down if they are trying to avoid a particular reaction!

- **Trust your spouse's heart**. Wow! A tall order but it is important. Very early in our marriage, my husband said to me, "I will never do anything intentionally or maliciously to hurt you." I heard him, but of course then came the tests. A couple of them I did not pass, as I forgot to use this filter of his heart intention. I usually found out after, that it was a fact, what I perceived as intentional was definitely not. He was usually hurt that I thought that he would want to hurt me. It is similar to a child who has been physically abused and someone comes over them and raises their hand. That child might reflexively duck, in anticipation of a blow, when the person was only reaching for something. Sometimes, our past experiences make us not want to totally trust someone, but when persons have proven that they "have your back" and would be more looking to protect you than to hurt you, you have to let down your defences and trust them. This trust in relationships keeps the communication lines open.

- **Individuals communicate differently**. I am the one who analyses my feelings quickly maybe as a result of training as a counsellor and years of practice. Then I want to express them. My husband usually needs more time. It is not that he does not want to talk about emotions but it takes him a longer time to even know what to talk about. I had to understand this. I want to place the cards on the table ASAP but it is more difficult for him to discuss especially sensitive issues – things that could affect a person's self-esteem; money-matters; other relationships and how it affects each, etc. So I liked to go into the deep stuff. My husband had to learn to talk about things he was not practiced in discussing prior to marriage. He has made super stride because of his teachable spirit and desire to enrich our relationship. Have you paused to study your spouse's communication style? What makes him/her tick and how to turn on their pipe of communication?

- **Be practical when it comes to communication**. Ask the How? When? Where? and Why? Questions. The how has to do with your manner of communicating verbally and non-verbally. Choice of words, tempering your emotions where necessary, lowering your voice, controlling your bodily reactions, would come in here. When, has to do with timing. None of us likes to be pounced upon to deal with especially troubling situations when we just walk through the door; when we are tired and/or hungry; when we are not feeling well; when we are already feeling overwhelmed. Asking your spouse if this is a good time to bring up a certain matter is thoughtful and allowing them to have a choice in the when will be appreciated. Where, has to do with location and who is present or not present. One has to be sensitive to this as some issues should not be brought up in front of children, guests, strangers, bosses, etc. What affects the bedroom should stay in the bedroom or at least be discussed in a private place where your spouse is able to listen and respond without thinking about those around him/her. The Why question has to do with motive. Some things can be dropped...left alone and not followed up. Some things we can deal with quietly by ourselves without dragging others into it. I therefore need to ask, why am I bringing up this topic/issue? Is it really important? How will it benefit this real-ationship if I do or if I don't?

- **Change Your Perspective**. My husband is actually the person who reminded me of this one. This is his contribution:

> *"In the early days of our marriage I did not like being instructed while driving. For example, being told where to drive, and which turn to take, or that there is an object in front of or behind the vehicle; the things that I thought were obvious to a capable driver. For me, it was a source of annoyance. However, I no longer get annoyed and when my wife asked why this no longer annoys me, my response was: "I have changed my perspective. At first, I used to interpret your instructions as questioning my ability to drive, or my skills of observation. Now I realize that it was being done from a desire to help, and to avoid ending up having to backtrack, spending more time in traffic, or avoiding an accident because of obstacles in the road." I have come to realize that there are the one-out-of-every-ten situations where her advice did in fact alert me to something I did not see just in time, or realized I was heading opposite to my planned destination. For this reason, I would rather cheerfully accept the nine times*

that I did not need the help, than miss the one time that I did need it."

Indeed, both of us have had to change our perspective and trust that the other has our best interest at heart. We also discovered that we did similar things, like instructing each other with the same motive of trying to help the other. It was not a commentary on our competence or even about weaknesses. It was rather out of a desire to support and strengthen our partnership. Husbands, as you build your real-ationship with your spouse, please accept her advice and help, even in areas where you may think you are an expert. Wives, the reverse is true, for example, even if you are an expert in the kitchen, allow your spouse to make comments and suggestions without taking offence. Even the best cook can try things differently and can be open to variety. After all, he may only be trying to be helpful.

Oftentimes, those who are trying to be helpful, when accused of being otherwise, will shut down and refuse to "interfere" and sometimes this spreads to other areas because the helpful spouse is now being viewed as meddling. This can rob you of valuable contributions which would enhance your real-ationship.

- **Change Your Style**. One of the things that often shuts down communication is our style of communicating. It is often not what is said, which might even be the truth but

HOW it is said that causes offence or hurt. This has to do with our tone of voice, body language, volume while speaking, distractedness, etc. Both men and women have to watch for "aggression", "belittling", "sarcasm" in their tones.

Dealing With Infidelity

This is a difficult section to write about as much as it might be difficult for some to read. If you have had to walk through this issue of adultery and general unfaithfulness whether on your part or on the part of your spouse, it may be painful for you. Either way, infidelity is so damaging to intimacy in a marriage, that it feels like your heart was ripped out! It has been difficult for me, as a counsellor, watching and listening to the devastating effects of how one experiences a sense of betrayal when his/her spouse goes to another; how the nature of that marriage changes from trust to distrust; the fears that enter especially of communicable diseases and the confusion of now having to deal with self-esteem issues which were not present prior to the discovery. From the outset, let me state that adultery is like a blunt force trauma which can result in the death of your dreams for a happy marriage. It is an enemy force that comes up against you and your spouse. Though there may be memories of pleasure in an affair, it is truly like taking fire into your bosom or walking on coal, as the wisest man Solomon said. (Proverbs 6:27-33)

What should we do if we find ourselves being tempted or having fallen? Deal with your *illegal connections.* Another term for this could be Toxic Relationships or Unhealthy Soul Ties. There is a dynamic that happens between people that goes way beyond a physical bonding or what we might call "chemistry". This is a linking in a deep emotional bond that should only be happening between you and your spouse. If it happens with anyone else in like manner, it usually brings a deep conflict within the individual, and some spouses can pick up that the connection once felt between them is no longer the same. Strange behaviours begin to appear, e.g. secretive phone calls and texting happening after bedtime. A spouse is no longer permitted to answer the other's phone, and there is no legitimate explanation that can be given. No longer wanting to spend time at home or to take out the other for no apparent reasons. We could list so many other changes that make a once trusting spouse become suspicious of the other's actions. So how does one give up such an illegal connection and break this toxic soul tie, remembering that a soul tie could continue even if the affair is said to be over? Kris Vallotton shares some signs that you have an unhealthy soul tie. [https://moralrevolution.com/7-signs-of-an-unhealthy-soul-tie/]

> *You have left a relationship (maybe long ago), but you think about the other person obsessively (you can't get them out of your mind)...*

When you have sex with someone else (hopefully your husband or wife), you can hardly keep yourself from visualizing the person you have a soul tie with...

You defend your right to stay in a relationship with the person that your soul is tied to, even though it is negatively affecting or even destroying the important relationships in your life (husband, wife, kids, leaders, etc.)

[https://moralrevolution.com/7-signs-of-an-unhealthy-soul-tie/

It's not that there has not been an attempt at breaking the unhealthy bond, or the severance might have taken place – communication ceased, no getting together with, and no physical contact, but there is still this "attachment" felt to this illegal connection. *Kahlia Hayes puts it this way:*

A soul tie is often the strongest when the relationship ended against your will or if you shared extensive years in a relationship with a particular person.

It seems as if your emotions have gone out of whack. You are not quite sure what to do with yourself if you have to go on without this "connection". Thoughts of crossing boundary lines leading to danger keep bombarding your mind. The temptation to throw caution to the wind just to be able to have this person when you want them, and in the way that you want them is greater. Sometimes it is not even that this person is treating you well. It is an unhealthy cord that keeps you attached and there seems to be a lock on your heart and the person is inside of it. Your illicit sexual endeavours now drive you to the brink of madness with the thought of never having that "stolen water" again. The person might have not been so "good" but when the time comes to let go, all of a sudden that person is being idolized and there is no one else quite like him/her. You may be asked by friends if you have bumped your head why you are behaving out of sorts. Where is the key to get free from all of this?

1. **Admit to Yourself, God and Your Spouse that You Did Wrong**. When a denial is pursued even after cold evidence, that hurts more, as reported by clients, than the actual affair. Some spouses are willing to forgive but are asking only for the truth to be told to them respectfully. That it happened; how it happened and other information that might be necessary for them to have in order for the offended party to move on.

2. **Reach out for Divine Help.** The truth is God is a bondage-breaker, and we can always count on Him to take us through. There are many who have attested to the fact that they really could not help themselves and when they turned to God with a "broken spirit", He heard their petition and answered them in their weakness, giving them strength to move on without this unhealthy soul tie. You should be expecting emotional sparks to be flying, and you will need to be praying for your wounded spouse at this time too. He/She will definitely need God's comfort and

support at this time. If children are in the home, they might have wind of what is taking place too. They need to be dealt with in wisdom, and prayed for so that insecurities do not arise and affect their own emotional and social development. The worst thing that could be happening now for the children is to be having a constant fear that their family unit could be split, and they no longer have the comfort of a home with both parents present. They too need God's intervention.

3. **Seek the Help of a Lay or Professional Counsellor.** In some cases, infidelity is a sign of a deeper problem and not the root cause. It is merely a symptom and until the root is dug up, the symptoms remain. Although the episode goes dormant for a while, if you don't deal with the root, it is usually only a matter of time, and you are back with the same problem emerging. You may have to look at your family history and background. Your own upbringing – who you socialized with; what you learned from them; who you saw as a model/hero. What are your perceptions of males, females, and relationships? You really may find a lot to go after, and you do need someone who can help you to make sense of your life and bring objectivity to your situation. A counsellor is able to look at the whole forest while you might be distracted by a few trees. Counsellors are also able to help you to make an action plan to practice

thought-stopping techniques and behaviour modification strategies.

4. **Having an Accountability Partner.** For many persons, unless they have someone to whom they are accountable, they only make it through to victory for a while and afterwards, without someone to check up on them, even to give encouragement, they fall. Those who are serious about walking upright morally, usually need such a person who is given the right to call them any time and ask them any question about their life especially in this area of struggle. In unusual cases, one's spouse is chosen as that accountability partner. Some spouses can stand strong in this role but not all, especially if the struggling spouse is having a setback.

5. **Cut off All Communication with the Other Party in the Affair.** This tends to be the strongest area of temptation – to keep a link going with the other party, pouring out their woes to each other about having to be apart. This is not healthy and does not help in the process of a clean separation. It only stirs up desires to comfort and to share in many ways with each other. If you the struggling party had promised your hurting spouse that you have stopped communication, and he/she should find out otherwise, any trust that was being rebuilt might be wiped out and perhaps now, with no hope of returning.

6. **If you are the Victim**. Yes, you will feel like walking out and giving up on this partner who you feel has betrayed you. But please do not make any hasty decisions before checking if this is a mistake that will not be repeated. There is always the need for forgiveness since forgiveness helps you more than it does the person you need to forgive. Sometimes it was genuine blindness, like not paying attention to an attraction to him/her and thus avoiding alone moments with the individual. It might be a one-off moment of weakness that he/she is very repentant about. If your spouse wants the marriage and is truly asking for your forgiveness, you can decide to forgive although your emotions might not be anxious for reconciliation and business as usual in the marriage. The **offending party** needs to be patient. Although you may want to be assured that you are forgiven and want to jump back into all aspects of the consummation of the marriage, whether male or female victim, they usually need time. This time is to deal with the shock of the "betrayal"; the disappointment of knowing that someone else was messing with what belongs to them; the reality that someone has intimate knowledge, through sex, of their partner, a knowledge that they thought was shared only between them. Outsiders might have been privy to this information and the victim feeling embarrassed and humiliated – as if being laughed at by

those who know. Here's a reminder to the offended spouse. You did not cause the infidelity; your spouse made a choice. There might have been extenuating circumstances that led to the spouse weakening but he/she made a choice.

7. **If you are the Other Woman/Man**. You would have realized that a marriage was damaged as a result of your involvement with one partner. You should be feeling some amount of remorse especially if you understand the Golden Rule. The question should then come into your mind, "If I was in the shoe of the offended spouse, how would I be feeling / what actions would I want to take now?" Every woman should, unless they have made themselves callous, have an idea of how heart-broken they would be and every man, unless cold-hearted, should understand sometimes the violence a man feels when they find out that their prized "possession" has been tampered with.

8. **Drink from Your Own Fountain**. I was counselling a situation of temptation and I was reminded of the saying of the wisest man Solomon, who has written indisputable words of wisdom for our lives in all ages. In Proverbs 5:15-20 (NIV)

15 Drink water from your own cistern, running water from your own well. 16 Should your springs overflow in the streets, your streams of water in the public squares? 17 Let them be yours alone, never to be shared with strangers.

18 May your fountain be blessed, and may you rejoice in the wife of your youth.19 A loving doe, a graceful deer— may her breasts satisfy you always may you ever be intoxicated with her love. 20 Why, my son, be intoxicated with another man's wife? Why embrace the bosom of a wayward woman?

The term, "drink from your own cistern or fountain" could apply to married persons who are unfaithful as well as the person (even if single) who is in an affair. God has set it up that if we are "thirsty" and married, we should turn to our own spouse to meet our sexual needs and our deep needs for affection. Affection can come from various persons in our lives, but there is a level of affection that brings emotional attachment and a soul connection reserved for lovers. When we look to others outside of our marriage for this, we begin to cross a threshold, and if we pause and think about this, we will realize that we are being hugged in a way that only our spouse should. We are enjoying a romantic touch that should be delivered to us only by our spouse. We are spending excessive time with someone else while our spouse is "thirsty" at home languishing for some quality time with his/her own spouse.

When you begin to find pleasure in looking at or touching someone else's body, you are crossing a line that you should not cross and you need once again to be "intoxicated" (made drunk) in and by your spouse's love. Your passions should not flow over to another rather than your spouse. The fires that are kindled in the body should be lit by your own spouse and if being lit by another, you are in the danger zone! No matter how pleasurable, and stolen water does have a sweet taste (Proverbs 9:17), we are ultimately destroying ourselves, and the precious exclusive intimacy that should be shared only between a man and his wife.

The Problem of Pornography

Indulging in pornography is adultery! What?! Yes it is. Jesus' definition and description of adultery starts in the mind and the heart – "look at and lust" (Matthew 5:28).

> *but I say to you that everyone who looks at a woman with lust for her has already committed adultery with her in his heart. (Matt 5:28 - NASB)*

"Has already"? This means without even getting to the action. Many might not like this statement because which one of us would truly be "innocent", especially if we have looked where we should not have and have lusted? If we are to be real, however, we need to honestly search ourselves and deal with the "look", yes that look, and the "lusting" -- many times the images that we have in our minds when we see someone who we find attractive. The imagination can go wild but that is fantasy.

Many go one step further. They might not ever think of having sex with anyone else except their spouse, but looking at pictures of naked women/men or watching "blue movies" is not a problem to them. Using these pictures as a point of contact for the eyes to stimulate sexual excitement does not bother them; after all the images are not the "real thing" and are not live. However, Jesus' description would apply here. The truth is, another woman/man, whether in a photo, video or the movies is stimulating and fulfilling in you only what your spouse should. It only seems to create a problem when the spouse discovers these illicit materials on cellphones, in the form of magazines, pictures, DVDs. The statistics on pornography is alarming!

> *In 2016, people watched 4.6 billion hours of pornography at just one website (the biggest porn site in the world). That's 524,000 years of porn or, if you will, around 17,000 complete lifetimes. In that same time people watched 92 billion videos (or an average of 12.5 for every person on earth). Significance: So many people are using so much porn today that it is really impossible to tabulate. But understanding how much is consumed at just one site can at least help us see that this problem is nothing less than epidemic.*

> *At age 11, the average child has already been exposed to explicit pornographic content through the internet. 93% of boys and 62% of girls are exposed to internet-based pornography during their adolescent years [https://www.challies.com/articles/10-ugly-and-updated-numbers-about-pornography-use/]*

Such is the problem of viewing pornography, and this problem continues into marriage as an issue. Often the user is thinking that it is not a big deal and their partner is overreacting while the non-user (most times the female) is thinking that she is not good enough why he needs these "other women". Usually, in her mind, the porn-models/actors are looking more attractive and willing to do the things that she is uncomfortable doing, and sees sometimes as downright vulgar. Lest we hasten to think this person is a prude, this is not necessarily so. These could be women who are willing to experiment in the bedroom with their partner, but are convinced and convicted that certain activities, e.g. watching X-rated videos to enhance one's sex-play is not good for the marriage. I am in agreement with this stance. I will put one of my reasons in the form of a question: "While viewing these videos, what is there to safeguard the viewers from imagining being the person in bed with the actor/actress?"

I recall seeing a wife in a nightgown with pictures of naked women, of a different race, strewn all over it. I was a teenager and in shock. I asked her why she would have bought herself such a nightgown. Her answer was, "My husband bought it and asked me to wear it." Even at 18 years old, that sent off danger signals in my head. Even at that time, I was wondering who he was seeing when he looked at her; the naked ladies or her. Pornography is another form of not "drinking from your own fountain".

Image by **Sasin Tipchai** from **Pixabay**

CHAPTER FOUR

THIS THING CALLED SEX!
BUILDING REAL INTIMACY

"Your spring water is for you and
you only, not to be passed around
among strangers.
Bless your fresh-flowing fountain!
Enjoy the wife you married as a young
man!
Lovely as an angel, beautiful as a
rose—don't ever quit taking delight in
her body.
Never take her love for granted!"
[Proverbs 5:17-20 (MSG)]

So God made sex. Selah (pause and think about this).

Although I have touched on the issue of sexuality in a previous chapter, I felt that an entire chapter dedicated to one of the top issues breaking up marital real-ationships was worth the space. If you jumped to this chapter before reading the others, welcome to the club of curious, excited- about- the- topic- of- sex- beings. Read on, but don't forget that knowledge of sex without balancing it with information in other critical areas of a relationship, could make you lop-sided and toppling in the relationship. Don't forget that marriages that were experiencing great sex have failed too. We therefore need all the information in all the areas to make our real-ationships work, that is, in order to have true intimacy.

I have had to counsel many formally and informally (too broken to come in for counselling) on this topic. I can't describe the pain that these individuals experience when they are failing in this area of their marriage, especially when issues of dysfunction crop up. Yours might be a great experience, but still read for the information. Some might not reach to a counsellor, but they might reach a breaking point and decide to confide in you. At least be able to point them to some answers and let them realize that they are not alone. We have wrongfully made sex, the be-all and end-all in marriage but it is not! There are so many other precious aspects of relating to someone. Persons in real-ationships recognize this and strengthen other areas while working on issues of dysfunctionality.

What is sex?

I could hear someone thinking, what a basic question. Even a small child has some idea of what it is but do they? Are you fully aware of what it is, i.e. what makes it different between human beings and when the dogs do it? Are we able to guide others into the realities that we are about to discuss about this thing called sex? This chapter is not about the genders, male and female, but about that activity that brings two people together in what seems like irresistible passion, often leading to procreation and the population and continuation of the human kingdom. It's that activity that has been responsible for the rise and fall of many kingdoms; the deposit for brokering many personal, national and international deals; the glue that keeps many together in unwholesome relationships; the cause of murders and suicides. It is powerful. It's this thing called sex.

Sex is shorthand for sexual intercourse and other forms of sexual stimulation. We also call males and females the two sexes.

Though sex is often considered a dirty topic, it's pretty important: without sex, there'd be no people, or animals for that matter. [https://www.vocabulary.com/dictionary/sex]

Why should sex be considered a dirty topic, and one that some parents might not want their old enough children to read about in a book like this? It has a lot to do with the **perversion** of what God has created. It does infuriate me somewhat, to think that God created something so beautiful for a male and a female to enjoy in the context of a marriage, and as a result of sin, the human race has turned it into all types of 'things' that God never intended. So we have related to sex, things like rape, abortions, human trafficking, prostitution, molestation, pornography, and all forms of perversion, too long a list to mention. What God has created and labeled "good", we now have to add to some forms of it, the description, "dirty" or "evil". Pastor Mark Driscoll in an article in Fox News, *What the Bible Really Says About Sex*, wrote:

> *Sex is a selfish act, a conquest of personal fulfillment. That's the mindset of most people in our culture regarding sex—even if it's only subconscious. For the most part, our society celebrates the process of hook up, shack up, and break up.*
> *All you have to do is take a moment to observe the way sex is communicated in our culture.*
>
> *Thousands of articles are churned out on how to cope with a past of multiple partners and how to find the next one.*
>
> *Porn is a massive industry, generating $10 to $14 billion annually in revenues...*
>
> *It also explains why sex trafficking is a $32 billion global industry, 45,000 to 50,000 young girls are trafficked in the United States every year, and why one in 12 youths experience sexual victimization, including sexual assault and attempted or completed rape.*
>
> *The problem, however, is not sex. It's us.*

One of the big mistakes we have made as human beings is the way that we view this activity – as merely physical. So I have a physical urge, leading to a physical act with someone and I satisfy that urge, and can move on if I choose to with no regard for the other person. I believe this is a myth. We have swallowed a lie!

Reason? **Sex is more than a physical act**! This is speaking of sex between humans. Sex as laid out in Scripture speaks about an exposure of one's soul to another; a deep intimate knowledge of another through such an act that could change each life forever. It is the joining, if you please, of spirit, soul and body. One triune person meeting another triune person in an act that bonds them together, not just in that moment, but if/when they walk away, they take a part of that person with them and vice-versa.

What brought this home profoundly to me was reading the Scriptures. I had always been taught that marriage makes two people become "one flesh". This is true. But what was left out, was that it was the sexual aspect of the marriage that made them one flesh. Therefore, upon reading another Scripture about sex with a prostitute, my eyes opened to a reality. Even when you have sex with a prostitute and never see that person again, the two had already bonded themselves. Let's examine this passage in 1 Corinthians 6:16:

When you join yourself to a prostitute, you become one with her in body. Don't you know this? Scripture says, "The two will become one." (Genesis 2:24 also) – NIRV

To what is this writer referring? What does Genesis 2:24 say?

For this reason a man shall leave his father and his mother, and be joined to his wife; and they shall become one flesh (NKJV)

What? Marriage and prostitution being put in the same context? Its results being the same, though one is sanctioned and the other is not? Yes, prostitution is not marriage, but it illegally does the same as marriage was meant to do. Sex is not something to play around with, and this is what we have to help young and older persons to understand. For further understanding of the topic, let us examine what sex is NOT, and what it IS INTENDED TO BE, as well as WHAT COULD GO WRONG even in the right context.

What Sex is Not

✓ *Not About Me – Meant to be a selfish act*

While growing up, what I saw (I was exposed early to pornographic material), and what I heard, gave me the impression that sex was about "getting". It was about me needing or wanting something from someone else. Many movies also portrayed the moving of two people towards each other as something that at least one was going after, for himself/herself. In other words, it was not usually about the other person – wanting to meet their need and therefore willing to wait, even if they have a need; putting the other person's welfare ahead of their own – an unselfish act. What was often portrayed was sometimes watching a person being punished because he/she was not meeting "my need". It was all about the individual with the need. If the other was not ready, was not interested, was not well, was under-age, belonged to someone else, it did not matter, as long as the person who desired sex had his/her need fulfilled.

✓ *Not About Power – Meant to subjugate others*

I have always pondered especially the issue of rape. The majority of perpetrators don't have a sexual need that someone else could not willingly supply. The rapist could have just come from a context where he was getting sex freely and go and rape someone. This then is not about a need for sexual release but a need to show power or force. The victim is usually someone who seems vulnerable, helpless, out of his league. The rapist's own feelings of inadequacy and insecurities in relationships propel him to prove something to himself. He is in control and women have to do what he wants them to do. Intimidation and violence often accompany this act. He does not have to feel anything towards the victim. The victim could be a stranger but somehow represents an easy victim that he could use to prove a point to himself. If known to him, sometimes it is wanting to send a message to his victim that she is not better than him, because he can subjugate her to get whatever he wants from her. This was never what sex was intended to be. A wanting to prove a point; send a negative message, intimidate and drive fear into another.

The controversy goes on re the issue of marital rape. Can there be such a thing? A person could feel raped in the context of marriage, if the person feels that her partner is using sex to prove a point of power or control, and it has nothing to do with consummation of their love and devotion to each other. It has been brought to my attention that in some of these unions, while the activity is going on, the domineering party does not even look at the other participant and even if he does, there is no tenderness in the eyes but more of anger and coldness. Can we see how then in such a situation someone could feel disconnected from her partner; a feeling of having sex with a stranger? Dr. Noam Shpancer, professor of psychology and a practicing clinical psychologist in an article in Psychology Today titled, Why Do We Have Sex' has this to say:

> *If someone touches your genitals clumsily, or when you're not ready or do not want to be touched, the contact will be painful, offensive, and disgusting, not exciting and pleasurable. [https://www.psychologytoday.com]*

✓ *Not About Fear – Meant to feel secure with children*

Pedophiles fall into this category. They tend to feel more confident having sex with children and are turned on by their youth and innocence. Pedophiles usually have some deep-seated insecurity in their adult intimate relationships, and sometimes they don't have adult relationships because of these insecurities. Children seem to them to be a safe place. Children would not have knowledge of what sex should be like, and therefore would not be comparing them sexually to other partners. Their innocence is appealing because it feeds into the perpetrator's need to make a fresh start, often to prove to himself that he is capable of sexual intimacy – he is not being censored based on his sexual performance or ability to act the role of an adult!

Females are guilty of this too, by initiating young boys/girls into sex. An article was written on the topic of female sex predators in the Jamaica Observer:

> *May 12, 2019, KINGSTON, Jamaica — It was reported on Tuesday that between 2013 and 2018, a total of 22 women were arrested for having sexual intercourse with boys under 16 years old. [**http://www.jamaicaobserver.com**]*

✓ *Not About Boosting My Self-Esteem – Meant to be shared with as many in order to build my confidence.*

One of the lies that men have often swallowed is the belief that there is something superb about them if they can boast of having sex with a thousand women. Wow! This wow for me means trouble and leaves a lot of questions to be asked. Where is this person's commitment? To which one/ones would and could he be deeply committed? King Solomon truly had one thousand women in his life, but his life ended up being empty and futile. How did his escapades help him to be satisfied in his life?

Being able to sleep with many women even if one feels that he is the perfect lover is like chasing after the wind, trying to meet a need that more and more women won't.

✓ *Not Masturbation – Meant to be a solo act*

One of the reasons given for discouraging masturbation is that it is a solo act. The truth is sex was never meant to be a solo act. In the act of masturbation, even if one is fantasizing about being with another intimately, it is not in reality giving to anyone else. It is consuming the pleasure upon self. No one else benefits. There is no giving taking place. During the act of masturbation, the individual is caught up with himself/herself. This individual manipulates his own body and/or mind to fulfill his own desire. One may ask here, so isn't a child who discovers the pleasure of manipulating his/her organs giving to themselves, when he/she is too young to be involved with another in the sexual act? Whereas a child might be experimenting in order to discover how his body functions, adults are not usually doing the same. There are adults who after marriage continue to masturbate because they have formed the habit and who knows someone's body and which button to press for stimulation more than that individual? Is sex made for individual consumption?

✓ *Not About Dealing with Loneliness or Boredom – Meant to fill an empty space*

There is a song that says, "You're looking kind of lonely girl, would you like someone you can talk to. I'm feeling kind of lonely too so if you don't mind, can I sit down here beside you…Would you mind, sharing the night together?" *[Artist. Dr. Hook & The Medicine Show; Album: Pleasure and Pain, Released: 1978, Songwriter(s): Ava Aldridge & Eddie Struzick]* From this songwriter's perspective, the answer to loneliness is sleeping together on a one-night stand. How many with this illusion of a night of fulfillment have after meeting a physical need, end up resenting themselves and their sex partner? They often don't want to see that person again; give wrong number; politely promise to see each other again knowing deep down that nocturnal escapade went nowhere. They are returning to where they started – lonely.

✓ *Not About Punishment – Meant to teach others a lesson*

Those who have had the joy of a healthy sexual relationship within the context of a mutual love relationship, cannot even imagine sex being used as punishment. We all know however, the horror story of soldiers, in the time of war, who use sex, which is actually rape, as a punishment for their female enemies. They use it to humiliate them. They see their sexual organ as a weapon to chasten, demean, degrade and humble their enemies. They watch their victims cower in fear and hope to die while being chastened in this manner. Some create such atrocities, using sexual activities against their enemies that they are, when caught, brought to justice for crossing certain lines. Have children been born under these circumstances?

There are individuals who are sadists and get a kick out of creating pain through the act of sex. If their partner does not experience physical or even psychological pain, then it is not good sex for them. This is not about "rough" sex which both parties may enjoy. This is about, as the saying goes, "what is one man's meat is another's poison".

Persons have become sexually involved sometimes to pass on a disease. It has been chronicled that persons with HIV, in their anger towards the one who gave them this disease, have also had unprotected sex with others, not caring to pass it on, with the hope that someone else will feel the pain that they are feeling for being given a "life sentence".

Sex should not be used as a part of a Token Economy system – rewards and punishment system. If you are a good boy/girl today and are on your best behavior, then you will be able to have sex with me but if not, no sex for you. Sex within a marriage is not something that someone possesses and should withhold or release depending on if they are pleased with their partners behaviour for the day. Withholding and defrauding your partner is really a far cry from what God intended it to be.

✓ *Not About Filling an Absent Mother/Father Gap*

Dr. Margaret Paul in an article, "Are You Using Sex For the Wrong Reasons?" expresses the following:

> *If your need for physical "mothering" was not met as a baby, then you may actually experience confusion between sexual desire, and a deep need to be taken care of. In other words, you may subconsciously be sexualizing your need for this kind of care.*
>
> *[https://www.mindbodygreen.com/0-17089/are-you-using-sex-for-the-wrong-reasons]*

I think of how many babies were born unwanted; how many intimate relationships were formed and did not last; how many marriages were entered into and the two experiencing such magnitude of pain; how many of these marriages were broken and how many people have lived with great regrets; all because of a "mother wound" or a "father wound". This is a serious wound that each of my readers, if you have such a wound and it was not properly processed, need to pause and think about it, and also act to deal with it. Sexualizing your need for an unmet nurturing and bonding relationship with your parent(s) in the past could have been at the root of your relationship woes as you entered your adult life. In such cases, the male or female, run into intimate relationships, giving sex to get love but not just the love of a mate, but incessantly seeking to fill a gap and a need that the other partner can never fill. They want too much sex (trying to fill a bottomless pit in their souls) or very little sex (wanting instead just to be cuddled). Both scenarios lead to issues in a marriage.

I can recall having to deal with a situation with a young man who immediately after hearing of the loss of a loved one, turned on an office worker, seeking to sexually stimulate her. He was using sex in this context to soothe his pain and to deal with his grief.

✓ *Not About Feeling Sorry for Another Person*

This is where many ladies lose it. Some "sad story" guy comes along; treated badly by all the ladies before in his life; life has dealt him some wicked blows and now he wants the comfort of sex. He manipulates her by his "sad stories" until she gives in to his need for "comforting". The truth is she is mistaking pity for love. She now feels like his Saviour – she is the only one who understands him, and she will never do to him what the others have done. It won't be long before she discovers that this was not love to begin with; that this "sad story" experience was based on a lot of baggage that this individual has carried, blaming everyone else and refusing to get help.

The person giving in to this act sees having sex with the individual as an act of mercy. It appeases something in the "sad story" victim and calms his insecurities about her love for him. The truth is, they both need help to unravel themselves from these kinds of encounters.

✓ *Not About Satisfying My Curiosity and Need to Experiment with My Body*

This is where especially young people need to be vigilant. They are at the stage of curiosity and feeling a need to experiment. I heard one young person say recently, "I want to taste it (sex) before I die". This was not the first time that I was hearing this statement. Sex is however, not like ice-cream. Let me taste and see if I like it or not, because it involves someone else and their own emotions. Since it bonds you spiritually to someone else that you might not care to be bonded to, you may want to think again. Even if it is "body sex" and you keep your emotions out of it, that is not always true for the other person who feels they have given a "sacred" part of themselves to you, and expect some kind of commitment from you having done so.

Wouldn't it be safer then, with an emotionally detached prostitute where you would not run that risk? Remember that sex is not just a physical act as pointed out at the beginning of this chapter. It was not intended either to be only that. There was one young lady a few years ago who had this approach. She was now a young adult and said to herself, "I might as well give up my virginity to see what all of this "excitement" over sex is about." She said when it was over; she despised the young man. She ended up with a "blah" feeling, questioning if this was all that there was to it, and as a result did not pursue any relationships with the opposite sex because, in her mind, there was nothing to which she could look forward. Nothing else was attached to this encounter except curiosity.

What Sex is Intended to Be

It is crucial before entering a marriage to understand what sex was meant to be. Sex is in the top reasons for marital breakup and therefore must be given careful attention and understanding. Tempers have flared, all types of abuses have been meted out, and people have walked away from a potentially good union, because of high frustration resulting from a lack of understanding on the side of one or both partners re this topic. So what was sex intended to be? What did the creator of sex, God Himself, have in mind when He unveiled this pleasurable activity to the first man and woman?

> Dr. Noam Shpancer has this to say:
> Good sex is learned; you have to work for it. It does not show up on its own. And it is not just about you alone. Sexual pleasure, it seems, is set up, operated, defined, and organized by external factors.
> [https://www.psychologytoday.com]

Sex also means different things to the genders and at different stages of life to each gender. Men and women are different in many ways when it comes to sex.

> "Men often start out being body centered," says University of Hartford adjunct psychology professor Janell Carroll. "But that changes later on. As men reach their 40s, 50s, and 60s, their relationship becomes more important."

*Richard Carroll has been counseling couples with sexual issues for
more than two decades. He says "Women actually become more
like men over time in that often, early on, sex is about initiating,
developing, strengthening, and maintaining relationships, but in a
long-term relationship they can actually focus on pleasure."
[https://www.webmd.com/sex-relationships/guide/why-people-
have-sex#3*

When it is understood what sex was meant to be, both genders
will be able to enjoy more fulfilling sexual encounters as this act of
marriage will not be viewed as "junk food" that tastes good, but
would be destroying our spiritual and emotional health in the
process. Sex will not be treated as grabbing a bite after driving
through a drive-through restaurant but rather having 3-course
meals (learning to dine) as a practice and having some fast-food
now and then. So sex is meant to be:

✓ *A Bonding Between a Man and a Woman*

This is the ultimate tie in the relationship. It allows a wife and
a husband to feel a connection with each other beyond the
emotional connection that they have been developing. It becomes
a celebratory act of their love that is not a one-off occasional
connection, but as often as both persons desire this celebration. I
don't know of any other act within a marriage that brings the two
people's bodies, souls and spirits interlocked in the highest form of
connection, producing vulnerability and a level of abandonment
that truly makes two people naked in every way with each other.

✓ *The Glue Within the Marriage*

I once heard someone say that 'God, knowing that marriage would be difficult, threw sex into it as brawta' (a great deal that comes as an extra benefit or blessing). We have often heard too that making up is sweet after a conflict when the two come together in sexual intimacy. Somehow the conflict divides and disconnects the two. Lovemaking (the term I prefer to use), brings back that connection especially when the conflict has been or is being resolved, apologies have been said and commitment to the relationship has been re-established.

✓ *The Means by Which Love Children Could be Produced*

I have chosen the term "love children" because I strongly believe that this was God's intention – that children be produced in the context of a love relationship that has been sealed through marriage. The love of both parents that brought them together in the act that produced these children, will be the same love that celebrates their arrival and covers them in their growing years. When they lovingly compare their own qualities and features seen in each child, it reminds them that love created that lovely mix. They can laugh about it and sometimes seek each other's counsel, especially when dealing with a fault within the child that reflects their own weakness. The blame game does not come into play here. Having recognized that none of them as parents is perfect, they now, together attempt to train up each child in the way that he/she should go.

✓ Giving to My Partner in Order to Meet Their Need

Most times when we hear persons expressing a desire for sex it is expressed more as a "I want something"; "I want her/him"; I have to get something tonight", "One way or another I have to get it from her/him". The theme is usually the individual with the desire wanting to get something; the emphasis is not on giving and a focus on how I am getting myself ready to pleasure my partner. There is a verse in the Bible that always amazes me and says something to me of how God thinks. Deuteronomy 24:5:

> "When a man takes a new wife, he shall not go out with the army nor be charged with any duty; he shall be free at home one year and shall give happiness to his wife whom he has taken."

> [Deuteronomy 24:5 – New American Standard Bible]

For some reason, I have hardly heard much mention of this Scripture, especially on what the focus should be within the year. It might not be practical in our age for the male or female to take one year off. However, it is the reason that jumps out at me. "…and shall give happiness to his wife whom he has taken." This is the purpose for taking off one year! Our cultures have taught us the other way around. That sex is about the male and the woman's focus is to be on giving him pleasure, so he won't be tempted to go outside of the relationship. Many times the focus is not on how the male's performance is pleasurable to the female. Some couples would not even approach this topic so the female partner learns to "endure sex". It is her duty to make him happy, so even talking about her lack of enjoyment might offend him.

This section is however, to emphasize the focus of our lovemaking. It should be about giving. If each person's focus is on giving, then both should be receiving and having a sense of importance in the process. Giving means *to present voluntarily and without expecting compensation; bestow; to grant (permission, opportunity, etc.) to someone; to set forth or show; present; offer; to furnish, provide, or proffer; to produce, yield, or afford; to relinquish or sacrifice; to apply fully or freely.* [Dictionary.com] These definitions are all about focusing on the other person.

There are times when one partner might not have had lovemaking on his or her mind. The thought of that activity at the time might be a struggling one. Sometimes the person is tired, distracted, frustrated, upset; just not feeling up to it. Here is how giving works. (a) The person who does not have the need at the time might have to make a sacrifice to meet a need, the need of their partner. Persons who have made such a sacrifice have often surprised themselves, realizing that they ended up enjoying and being fulfilled in the process. Some felt better after because love-making relieved some stress and was a pleasant distraction. (b) The person with the need may have to give up that opportunity in the interest of the partner who might definitely not be feeling well, etc. It might be hard to hear "No" but that denial should not be taken as rejection. In a real-ationship, either partner should have the freedom to say "No" at times. When it causes concern, is if it's a consistent denial over a long period of time and there is no sincere explanation. This now becomes an issue for the couple to sit and discuss and where necessary, introduce professional intervention.

Unresolved conflicts, internally or within the relationship can affect, especially the female in this context. This is the amber or red light to indicate that it is time to address the issues.

✓ *Showing Love & Feeling Loved by Your Partner*

There is something about lovemaking and the celebratory aspect of this activity, that reassures each person of the love and commitment of the other. It has been said that 'women will give sex to get love and men will talk love to get sex'. In a real-ationship, no one should use sex in a manipulative manner. When each person feels desired and desirable, and both express this in their real-ationship, each person feels loved. A man does feel loved when his wife initiates lovemaking. He does not view this as her being less than a lady, but as an expression of her love for him – she wants me! When a wife knows that her arms means everything to her spouse, and he has his full drink of pleasure only from her; she feels loved – he wants only me. Yes, when sex is ministered from a genuine emotional place of giving pleasure to one's spouse, it says "I love you".

✓ *For Pleasure*

Yes. Simply for the pleasure of it within the context of a committed marriage relationship. Pleasure however does not just come about. Two people have to work at it. Each has to study his/her partner and look at ways to enhance the bedroom experience. Couples who have been married for a while will admit that the initial bang of the honeymoon, or getting beyond the curiosity to the actual experience and excitement of finally bonding with the love of their life, sex can become mundane, routine and for some, dull. It does not have to however, if the partners are committed to exploring and being creative when it comes to this act. There are books that have been written to assist re this topic. One such book that had prepared me for marriage was Tim and Beverley LaHaye, The Act of Marriage. The LaHayes put forth some ideas re what sex means to each gender. To the male they purport that it satisfies his sex drive; it fulfills his manhood because he possesses a stronger ego than the woman; it enhances his love for his wife; it reduces friction in the home; it provides life's most exciting experience. For the woman, it does some similar things: it fulfills her womanhood; it reassures her of her husband's love; it relaxes her nervous system; the ultimate experience;

This is where communication (verbal and non-verbal) must take place between the couple. Your partner is not a mind-reader. Communicating through the process is not "dirty talk" and if you are religious, you don't need to feel as if you are sinning because of expressing your pleasure or desires in the process. He/She will need to hear from you and be given guidelines, especially since nothing is just automatic. Like a map, they will need directions, whether to go north or south; to turn left or right and at the right time to take such a turn. Each through communication should know where they would like to stop on the way – where to park for a while. Especially for females, they like to end the journey by pausing to connect emotionally, especially if they were not feeling that connection before. They usually want to cuddle for a while. To bask in the afterglow. A loving husband, even if this is not a need for him, would pause to give in this way to his partner. Dr. Noam Shpancer in an article, *Why Do We Have Sex?* wrote:

You and your lover do not bring your sexual pleasure to the relationship. You get sexual pleasure from the relationship. Your body parts do not charge the relationship with sexual pleasure. The interaction charges your body with sexual pleasure. Pleasure is not derived from the physical stimulation of the genitals or from the possibility of giving birth to the next Bill Gates. In its most fundamental sense, sexual pleasure is derived from the synchronized cooperation between people. The whole of human contact is larger than the sum of its participating individual parts—possessing better resilience, greater wisdom, and deeper delights. Therefore, we seek that whole everywhere, including in sex.

[https://www.psychologytoday.com/us/blog/insight-therapy/201204/why-do-we-have-sex]

Understanding the Differences Between Male and Female

There are two analogies that are apt descriptions of the difference in sexual response between the sexes. The first is one of an electric switch. The male would be likened to this one. The male is turned on mainly by sight so he can see something, e.g. his spouse getting ready for bed and becomes turned on. One click. The female is like dimmers which could be in the form of a rotating or sliding knob on the wall to turn the light on. You gauge the intensity of the light by moving this knob which will decide how dim or bright you want the room to be. Usually it has to be done slowly to get the right gauge. The second analogy is an electric iron. It has to be gauged depending on the material it is going to be used on. Every fabric is not the same. Then on the same garment, you may have different types of fabrics. The person handling the iron has to know how to handle these variables, so the iron does not damage the more delicate sections or wrinkles are left in the fabric because it needed more intense heat. The person who designed the fabric knew that the users would need to know how to handle his creation. The user would have to have some knowledge of irons, the ironing process, the fabrics, when to apply moisture, etc.

Only the individual through communication, can help the opposite sex to understand what is felt, and at what point because bodies function differently. Interestingly enough, we even vary from one experience to another. It is amazing that what worked before does not always work the next time, so there is no real formula and this is what makes the journey exciting. Couples in a real-ationship enjoy the excitement of this exploration, and it keeps boredom and monotony away.

It saddens me to hear husbands in a demeaning manner telling their wife to go and learn how to make love. They are not speaking here of their partner going outside of the marriage, but to go and read books or Google new methods. This is so distasteful, as how God intended the sexual experience, like the soldier mentioned in the Bible, it was to be a year-long if you will, trip to paradise, enjoying all the sceneries along the way, stopping to smell the roses, parking and taking in the breath-taking views, teaching where there is an expert and enjoying the moments of learning together. The destination reached would be more fulfilling if both persons enjoyed the long or short journey.

What Could Go Wrong Even In The Right Context?

This is the section that not many persons want to read because of the pain and trauma couples have experienced, when the "machinery" does not work the way that it was expected to. Let me hasten to say that wherever the dysfunction is, it is not "You have a problem, go and fix it!" Rather, it is we have a problem, let's see how we can together fix this. This encourages the partner who might be experiencing the dysfunction to get the help needed as they are both in it together. So isn't sex automatic, like we see the lower animals perform. What could then go wrong?

Dealing With Sexual Dysfunctions

Many a couple has gone to bed broken-hearted, frustrated, angry, tempted to seek recourse outside the union and some in actual physical pain because one or both have had a dysfunction. This could happen at any stage of lovemaking. Didn't they know of this dysfunction before they came together? Not necessarily. Sexual dysfunctions, temporary or permanent, could crop up along the way and early, mid-way or later in the marriage. This is why the marriage vow is so important – for better or for worse, we are going to walk this thing through! These dysfunctions, although more common among older couples, usually because of degenerative health issues, many young persons have reported (or kept a secret out of embarrassment), the fact that they are not performing the way they wish to in the sexual encounter. What is sexual dysfunction? What are some of these dysfunctions?

Sexual dysfunction refers to a problem occurring during any phase of the sexual response cycle that prevents the individual or couple from experiencing satisfaction from the sexual activity. The sexual response cycle traditionally includes excitement, plateau, orgasm, and resolution. Desire and arousal are both part of the excitement phase of the sexual response.

*While research suggests that sexual dysfunction is common
(43 percent of women and 31 percent of men report some
degree of difficulty)*

*[https://my.clevelandclinic.org/health/diseases/9121-sexual
dysfunction]*

The statistics report that almost half the amount of women
engaged in sexual intercourse express problems in this area and
one-third of men. Please note that these are the reported stats. I
wonder if there are many who have not reported theirs because it is
a taboo subject. Well this is the reason I am opening up the subject
in this forum to help you to understand that in the same way, other
parts of our body can dysfunction, e.g. we get a sprained ankle and
we cannot walk or do certain activities that depend on our mobility
like we used to; in the same way, our sexual organs or the part of
the brain that controls sexual response can pause or cease its
normal functions. What type of functions can be affected?

Types of sexual dysfunction

So a normally functioning sexual process would start with
persons having a desire for sex which is natural, and usually starts
around the time of puberty with many hormonal changes taking
place in the body. If someone at this stage of life and afterwards
has absolutely no sexual desires, or interest in sex, or if they started
out with this desire and now are at ground zero, then this is a sign
that something is wrong. One may have thought long and hard

about sex but when the time comes around, there is an inability to respond to attempts at arousal (no libido). Physically nothing happens. If it were to be drawn on a chart, your arousal pattern physically would not rise from zero. You would report absolutely no excitement during the act in spite of various attempts to stimulate you. A climax in this process is the ultimate goal. Those who have long delay or the absence of this goal would know that something is wrong too. For others, there might be pain during intercourse and there are no medical explanations. It is understandable that persons experiencing this, would want to stay away from this activity. I tried to explain it to one husband: "Consider having a deep cut and someone keeps sticking an implement into the cut bringing recurring pain; would you find pleasure in that?" Of course, his answer was no. We still had to address the causes of the dysfunction and look at ways to correct this.

What are the types, symptoms / signs of sexual dysfunction?

These can be placed in two categories based on gender. For the **men** there can be erectile dysfunction which is an inability to get or maintain once gotten, an erection. Some men are fine and can achieve this goal, but the problem comes afterwards. They might either not be able to ejaculate or it takes a long time in spite of his many efforts. There are others whose issue is not the fact of the ejaculating but the timing – it happens too soon and long before

THIS THING CALLED SEX! BUILDING REAL
INTIMACY

either is ready for it. All of these issues can bring about
tremendous frustration in the marriage.

For women, the top one would be an inability to achieve the
ultimate goal of lovemaking, climaxing (anorgasmia). I have
heard it described as similar to an aborted sneeze. Have you ever
felt like sneezing? Your nose burns, everything seems to be
building up to it but…nothing! You still could be feeling the
symptoms but…! Some women have reported that they have never
sneezed (had a climax), no matter what is done or how skillfully it
is done. To some readers, this might be a shock to you but to
many women it is a reality. Vaginal lubrication, especially for
older women and those experiencing menopause, creates issues for
them in the sexual act. What is worse however is the tightening of
the vaginal muscles disallowing intercourse (vaginismus).

What can be done to correct the problem?

Firstly, it's to find out what is causing it in the first place. Is
the cause a physical /medical one? Is it psychological or spiritual?
Physical causes may be similar for both genders.
www.my.clevelandclinic.org points out some physical and
psychological causes:

Many physical and/or medical conditions can cause problems
*with sexual function. These conditions include **diabetes**, **heart***
***and vascular (blood vessel) disease**, neurological disorders,*
hormonal imbalances, chronic diseases such as kidney or liver

*failure, and **alcoholism** and **drug abuse**. In addition, the side effects of some medications, including some antidepressant drugs, can affect sexual function.*

Psychological causes *— These include work-related stress and anxiety, concern about sexual performance, marital or relationship problems, depression, feelings of guilt, concerns about body image, and the effects of a past sexual trauma.*

[www. my.clevelandclinic.org]

The **spiritual causes** are not usually addressed. If you are around religious persons for a long time and especially those of previous generations, you would have heard some very conflicting views about sex. For example, I have heard well-meaning ladies declare that sex is only for procreation. If a young woman gets married with this mentality, after having out her lot, she would want to desist from this activity. The goal would have been met. We can imagine the pain, frustration and confusion, in the mind of one or both, if the husband wants to continue having sex as a natural part of their union. Some ladies have been discouraged from sexual experimentation with their spouse and especially about initiating sex because "Ladies don't do such things." Such women with old wives fables have discouraged their daughters from making their bedroom an exciting place. The husbands who attempt to be creative are viewed as unspiritual, carnal and pagan. Such persons have forgotten or misinterpreted the Scripture that says marriage is honourable in all, and the bed undefiled. (Hebrews 13:4)

Please don't take this lightly. This spiritual blockage and root cause has led to psychological problems and affected physical functioning even if the deceived spouse decides to surrender out of duty. Like someone not enjoying the job they do, they will make their bodies available, but might be absent psychologically and this is felt by their partner. Not wanting to be uncompassionate but to help you to understand what this feels like for such a husband; it feels like making love to a log – a piece of wood! This is not good for a marriage especially when having read above what marital sex was meant to be – a glue, a bonding, for pleasure and showing love for your partner. It has led to marital unfaithfulness, separation and ultimately divorce. Whereas each person is responsible for the choices they make, each partner would need to look at the root cause for each of their actions, and how such choices have/ are affecting their partner.

For the **woman**, when the problem of dysfunction is primarily physical/medical, there are practical solutions that can be applied. A physical exam which might include a pelvic exam and pap smear would be necessary to rule out any medical root causes. A prescription could be given to treat medical problems. At that point some medical professionals might ask other questions to do a proper evaluation and to make recommendations.

An evaluation of your attitudes regarding sex, as well as other possible contributing factors (such as fear, anxiety, past sexual trauma/abuse, relationship problems, or alcohol or

drug abuse) will help the doctor understand the underlying cause of the problem and make appropriate treatment recommendations.
[https://www.webmd.com/women/guide/sexual-dysfunction-women#2]

A physical root cause could be hormonal changes. These changes can affect the female around the time of menstruation, around the time of childbearing and with the onset of menopause.

Hormones play an important role in regulating sexual function in women. With the decrease in the female hormone **estrogen** *that is related to aging and* **menopause**, *many women experience some changes in sexual function as they age, including poor vaginal lubrication and decreased genital sensation.* *[https://www.webmd.com/women/guide/sexual-dysfunction-women]*

Vaginal lubricants have been a God-sent help to assist in reducing pain caused by friction. Menopausal or post-menopausal women need not worry. There is help. Have fun applying it. You can still enjoy intercourse.

Would you believe that ignorance could lead to many psychological and spiritual causes of sexual dysfunctions? Enlightening the couple's darkness on various issues could begin to set them free – the truth about sex, understanding how their bodies function differently, who created sex, what is healthy in the sexual process and that God sanctions sexual intimacy between a man and his wife purely for pleasure. Many women, especially if religious, need this information.

Especially a female therapist could suggest to her, ways that she could be creative along with her husband, including communicating during the sexual act. Sometimes simply helping the woman to be comfortable with her body, and using her husband to assure her / alleviating any anxiety about her looks and performance as his wife, can go a far way to remove some of the psychological blocks.

There are other issues that could be at the root of a female's sexual dysfunction, e.g. a history of sexual abuse; participation in the occult which demanded sexual religious rituals. This would need professional counselling as it impacted her deeply.

For **males**, the treatment is similar in that a lot depends on whether the root cause is physical, psychological or spiritual. Research suggests that low levels of the male hormone **testosterone** also contribute to a decline in sexual arousal, genital sensation, and orgasm. [https://www.webmd.com] This is a physical problem that could be addressed medically if the male will submit himself to proper examination, assessment and treatment. The male will need to look at other physical factors, such as whether or not they are using any form of drugs, and how these might be impacting on their sexual functioning. Some prescription drugs treating medical conditions and some medical conditions like diabetes, depression, benign prostatic hyperplasia (BPH), pain, and prostate cancer can lower libido.

A psychological factor for the male which must always be honestly examined, since it plays a part in his sexual arousal is his level of attraction for his partner. A man can be angry with his spouse and still desire her sexually, but when that attraction is not there, there might be problems in the area of performance. Medicinenet.com lists alcoholism, depression, fatigue, hypoactive sexual disorder, recreational drugs, relationship problems, fear of humiliation, sexual aversion disorder, systemic illness, testosterone deficiency, stress, lack of time, history of sexual abuse, and hormonal problems such as hyperthyroidism as possible causes of sexual dysfunction in men. For the treatment for erectile dysfunction they suggest:

> ... a change in lifestyle habits. Since many causes of erectile dysfunction are disorders in which lifestyle changes will have a positive effect, addressing these issues can be helpful. Therefore, regular **exercise**, a healthy **diet**, **smoking cessation**, and limiting alcohol consumption can all have an impact on erectile function. Lifestyle changes can also include the use of a more genitalia-friendly bicycle seat.
>
> [https://www.medicinenet.com/sexual_sex_problems_in_men/ article]

The most common form of ejaculatory dysfunction in men is premature ejaculation. Research has shown that approximately 20% to 30% of men will have premature ejaculation.

[www.medicinenet.com] This one is highly misunderstood by female partners. With premature ejaculation, through ignorance the female partner usually feels frustrated and resentful of her partner as this disorder is deemed as intentional the man is impatient to get to his goal and refuses to wait on her. The assumption is that he has control over his performance. Men, knowing the truth, have suffered from this accusation, and the diminished satisfaction and frustration that they too encounter, because this achievement of ejaculation was unpleasantly outside of their control. The "blame game" here often leads to more pain and increased anxiety in the male, exacerbating the situation. There are non-pharmacological ways to address this issue.

Psychologically, the male has to deal with anxiety if that is what is at the root of it. Counselling could help him here. Behind much of this anxiety is usually the fear of performance. The focus is on performance and it is this very focus that creates anxiety. He can do some simple bathroom exercises like while urinating, instead of releasing his urine in a flow as is customary, he can do a stop-start repeated exercise until he is finished urinating. This will help him in control of his pelvic area and strengthen his pubococcygeal (PC) muscles. You may read more on pelvic floor muscle training on [https://www.healthline.com/health/kegel-exercises-for-men]

This thing called sex that the young dream about, the elderly have memories about, and those in between have to work out, does not have to become a lifetime of disaster. Understanding the purpose of sex, building proper real-ationship with your spouse, including communicating openly about this activity in your marriage and together addressing any issues/dysfunctions that occur can go a far way in allowing this aspect of your marriage to be truly a dream come true.

CHAPTER FIVE

WE ARE FAMILY...BUT NOT BY BLOOD

"[Adoption] carries the added dimension of connection not only to your own tribe but beyond, widening the scope of what constitutes love, ties, and family. It is the larger embrace." - Isabel LaRossellini

The statistics show that there are an estimated 153 million children worldwide who are orphans [Worldwide Orphan Statistics - SOS Children's Villages *https://www.sos-usa.org/our-impact/childrens-statistics*]. Can you even wrap your mind around this number of children with no one to bond with? No one to call their own Mommy or Daddy?

Orphans Press Centre UNICEF –
https://www.unicef.org/media/media_45279.html
Jun 16, 2017:
- UNICEF and global partners define an orphan as a child under 18 years of age who has lost one or both parents to any

cause of death. By this definition, there were nearly 140 million orphans globally in 2015, including 61 million in Asia, 52 million in Africa, 10 million in Latin America and the Caribbean, and 7.3 million in Eastern Europe and Central Asia. This large figure represents not only children who have lost both parents, but also those who have lost a father but have a surviving mother or have lost their mother but have a surviving father.

Of the nearly 140 million children classified as orphans, 15.1 million have lost both parents. Evidence clearly shows that the vast majority of orphans are living with a surviving parent, grandparent, or other family member. 95 per cent of all orphans are over the age of five. [https://www.unicef.org]

It is very difficult for me to think of children without parents or without a loving substitute parent/caregiver knowing what children need for their full spiritual, psychological, social and physical development. I do believe that we have the answer to this predicament of the orphaned children worldwide. Those answers lie within our hearts – hearts of compassion towards those who are less fortunate.

I was always moved to foster / adopt children whether or not I had biological children. I was delighted to know that my husband had the same dream. We did adopt officially and unofficially and ended up taking care of, and supporting those who were taking care of wards of the state.

There are many myths regarding taking into your home a child that is not biologically related to you. I have heard that you will end up with an unhealthy child that will constantly disrupt your home, to that child growing up to become a criminal and turn around and take your life! These are some of the myths. I ask one question. Doesn't this scenario occur in natural families too? One of the top reasons given in my country for cause of murders is domestic violence. If checked out, it is not because of a foster/adoption situation. Blood-relatives can hate each other and carry serious vengeance in their hearts, that lead to emotional instability and household disturbances.

In an article in our local newspaper, *The Gleaner*, Feb. 20, 2018 titled, "More Foster Parents Needed; Several Children Waiting", one of our state ministers, Floyd Green, through this article was making an appeal. This appeal I would want to endorse since there are many children, even in my country, who long to be a part of a family they can call their own, and need to be healed from the many reasons and memories of being separated from their own biological parent(s).

The statistics also show that for the period of October to December 2017, the agency recorded a total of 4,195 children living in the residential child protection sector.

Of this amount, 1,265 children are living in children's homes, 269 are living in places of safety and 767 in foster homes.

He says he wants to see more Jamaicans opening up their hearts and homes to foster children.

Why Should We Adopt?

Adoption and fostering is a critical way to help some of the most vulnerable in society. It is heart-rending to see what happens to children who grow up in this system and are compelled to leave by age 18. Many times, they have ambitions like any other child within biological families, but because they often don't have anywhere to go, the predators are just waiting. They form relationships with these young girls with the hope that as soon as they can leave, (sometimes it is before age eighteen that they are enticed to run away), they can get them to come and live with them. These girls go into, many times, abusive environments that they are stuck in if they have nowhere else to go. They begin to have children and they are unprepared to be a parent or a spouse.

Shouldn't all children have a right to a loving home and family? If your answer is yes, then foster care /adoption is often the best vehicle to make this happen for children in need of such a loving home environment. I have seen couples who are unable to have a biological child and they would rather die childless and with that emptiness in their hearts and home of having a childless union, than to have fostered or adopted a child. Is it impossible for such a couple to love another person's child? Many times it does not matter to the child in need of that love that these are not their biological parents. They are happy to be chosen to be loved as their own child. I have heard it said, "It is not you who adopt a child; the child must adopt you." Here it is emphasizing the importance of choosing correctly the child who will bond with you. There is usually a trial period in which one can decide, including the child, if this is what they desire. Some are worried about the nature of the child since they, the couple, do not know the biological parents and their background. When we have biological children, we cannot swear for their nature either. So many characteristics are carried through our genes from previous generations. Biological parents are sometimes shocked at the type of child they have produced, whether in physical features or character flaws. Some amount of wisdom must be applied, agreed. As much research as possible re information that the agency has on the child is necessary. However, the "nature-nurture" debate has never stopped, and the conclusion is still up in the air. Are we who we are more by nature (what is within our genes and passed on to us through our parents)? Or, are we formed more by nurture (our environmental influences from all the social systems we are exposed to in our growing-up years.)

It is critical to the healing of the "mother-wound" and the "father-wound". Don't get me wrong. I am not here suggesting either that these kinds of wounds don't come when one is still living with his/her biological family, or that it will always be healed just by living within a foster/adoption environment. I am simply saying that where there has been abandonment by parents; all types of continuous abuse in the home; parents admitting that they are unable to provide the care that this child needs, and children being punished for even existing, it would be better for these children to be within a family where they can feel loved and accepted. Where their presence can be celebrated, and they are seen as a gift from God to that family.

The "mother-wound" and the "father-wound", having dealt with it growing up with the absence of a father in my life, and not knowing why he never took care of me and the many siblings I had in different nations, was a deep wound. It took years of informal counselling and the care of spiritual fathers to heal this wound. It took God's intervention to prove to me that He is the Good Father who never abandons His children and keeps His promises to them. Thank God for those interventions. What happens to those who don't get this help? I meet some in the counselling environment and some in the streets. The picture is not pretty. Many have been through painful and traumatic experiences, especially in relationships just searching for love and belonging. I have heard it said that some females give sex to get love. The males may talk about love to get sex, believing that sex will bring them what they are longing for. They get involved in gangs and cliques that were socially unhealthy. They end up doing drugs and some have been in and out of prison, running a wild and confused life. What they know of relationships has not been through wise counsel, but trial-

and-error and being taught as they run the streets. I did not end up in this way, but I am the first to admit that without the type of interventions I got early, it is by the grace of God that I did not.

It can fulfill your maternal and paternal instincts. Some females and males have medical issues why they are unable to conceive. Sometimes they are able to conceive but believe that the risk of passing on genetic health issues is too risky, and might opt not to have a biological child but still want to have children. It is sad that those who cannot for various reasons, opt never to fulfill their need for children when there is a wide open door to still be fulfilled by the laughter and joy of nurturing young lives. Those who have been brave enough to step out and to attempt to love another person's child, have found that a child can capture your heart whether you brought that child into the world or not. It has been said that you don't adopt a child; a child adopts you. This I have seen happen to a friend who has been an adoptive and foster parent for over two decades. One of her children was chosen because he chose her when she visited the Children's Home where he was resident. He ran to her and endeared himself to her. Now he is an adult and still living at home and working in the family business. He was abandoned as a small child. This lady's intervention allowed him to experience a mother's love and she to fulfill her maternal ability to nurture children. She never got married but her adult years and home have been filled with children, some for a short time but some until they have grown into adulthood.

My own home now is filled with this type of joy. I am truly grateful for a mother who was able to love other people's children; a brother who grew his step-child as if she was his own biological child; my foster-parent friend who took me with her to a Children's Home and started me on the journey even while single, of taking children into my home. One of these children became my godson and after twenty years, I am still his Mom. My intervention in his young life brought his Dad into the picture, and he was able to heal the "father wound" and the "mother wound". He is a father today and responsibly taking care of his son.

It has happened too that you may remain single but still want to nurture a child and believe that you could handle being a single parent and that it is better if a child has one parent than none at all.

This was my plan. If I did not get married, I still would have fostered or adopted. I have always loved children, beginning with my own nieces and nephews. From a teenager I took care of them, feeding babies, washing "nappies" which was what we used then before there were diapers. I took them to the movies while I was a teenager. As an adult, I always had children in my home. My foster-parent friend was once my flat-mate, so I encountered different children. Two of them became my god-children.

Ideally, I would not have wanted to be a single parent. However, I did not want to be just working for myself; building life for myself. I had so much to give and wanted to share all of this with children. I know that I would have been fulfilled even if I had to do it alone. I knew that it would have been challenging but I would have taken the chance. The children that I related to back then I built real-ationships with and taught them how to be real; to be themselves. It would be ideal to have both parents to do this, but one is better than none. It takes bravery to love someone else's child and courage to set aside some of your own dreams, and resources to pour your life into a child that carries none of your genes, but can reflect so much of your values later.

There is a biological relative with a child, but he/she is unable to take care of that child. This child gets to stay within the context of his/her biological relatives, something that each child needs, to have a sense of identity. To know where he/she came from. To know some of the reasons why he may look and act the way he does. Although I grew with my biological Mom, I was very enlightened when I finally met my biological father at the age of 18. I used to hear little things along the way like, I danced like him. When I finally met him and my estranged siblings, I could see what genes could do. Although I did not grow up with these siblings, and met some of them when they were in their forties, I was startled at how we resembled each other, not only physically but in habits, mannerisms, values, etc. My encouragement to you, if you have a relative with a child that he/she cannot nurture, that you seriously consider taking that child if you are able to. I encourage you to open your heart to help in such a situation.

There is a divine call to do so. As simple as tha,t and it could be that out of gratitude to God persons choose to give back to Him and/or society in this way. What a selfless reason to open one's heart to raise a child that is not biologically connected to you. Many have reported that they felt led by God to foster or adopt. Some were not thinking in this direction, but a situation came up when a child needed their help. After praying about the matter, the couple or single person felt a strong convictio,n and divine persuasion to take into their home a child /children that they did not bear. In some instances, they were planning on one and realized that there was a sibling. Their verdict, sometimes after much consultation was not to split them up. They adopted the sibling(s) too.

The Scripture is rife with exhortations to protect the orphans and helpless. God obviously has a "soft-spot" in His heart for those without parental nurture and protection. It would be His delight to see these children being embraced and legally secured in healthy families, who can be an extension and practical manifestation of His love for them.

Although not common, you could be divinely led to adopt someone over the age of eighteen. This would become your adult-child, and usually the purpose is for mentorship, coaching, discipling or filling some gap in that individual's life, which is necessary to propel them into their God-given purpose.

Jenene's Story:

How Fasting Helps Relationships

The Lord connected Mommy Maria and I through a mother-mentor relationship, and I see why because it has been the most effective in fulfilling a significant part of God's purpose in my life. There were other mentorship relationships that God used to develop different aspects of my life – professional and social - but then He decided that this time it would happen through a mother-daughter-mentorship relationship. I have been receiving mentoring and mothering which the Lord effectively used to heal wounds and scars from past relationships.

<u>My relationship before much fasting</u>

Mommy Maria would do things and instruct me with good intentions, but I would interpret them as negative actions and feel hurt about it. There was also a part of me that wanted to push her help away or keep her out of my life at points when I was going through my deepest struggles and needed help the most. This mother-mentor, God was truly using to deliver me from wounds and rejections that I experienced in different ways beginning in my childhood.

The Effect of Fasting

I commenced a 50-day, half-day fast deliberately because the number '50' represents jubilee in the bible, where persons who were in debt or slavery were freed from all those bondages in the jubilee years. I asked the Lord that during this fast to set me free from things that kept hindering my progress in life, relationships and just about everything. I told the Lord I was tired, as God was revealing to me some root causes of my wrong attitudes, mind-sets in my life that became hindrances and setbacks. He significantly used my mother-mentor to shed light in these areas, given her counselling and intercessory background. God was using her to bring deliverance, hope and encouragement. Although I was mindful of this, and we had a real and truthful relationship, I still found myself misunderstanding her motives and actions, based on the hurt from past experiences, and the negative reasons attached to some of these actions in past relationships. I instantly put Mommy Maria's action in the same category as the others. After our discussions I would find out that the intentions were wholesome and in my best interest. I have been learning not to judge a person's reason for their actions based on what others have done. Each individual should be judged on their own merit.

Through fasting, my spiritual eyes became opened and a lot of things that were clouded in my mind regarding this divine connection were becoming clearer. I realised that there was a devil working on my emotions and creating misunderstandings, blinding my eyes to what God wanted to achieve. There were times I reacted in a negative manner, not disrespectful, but ways that would make relating to me non-delightful, and while fasting I saw that Satan himself was using me to drive away the person from relating to me, because I was being testy. Fasting was the key needed to discern that this was a plan of the Enemy (Satan) to stop the work God wanted to do in me. I realised it was a plan to frustrate the process, and the impact that the mother-mentor relationship was to have on my life. I couldn't control my reactions through human effort nor go beyond surface thinking - I just took things at face value. Fasting helped me to see that my mother-mentor had a good heart, even though it hurt me when truth was presented, and balance was exercised. I realized that she would do exactly what any other mother has to do sometimes, which is to take actions that are in the best interest of her children, even when it hurts. I was learning how "tough-love" works.

Being 'adopted' as an adult is new and not a popular thin, but when God predestines something, He does it with a purpose even when it doesn't make sense to others. Well I discovered as the months went by why God made the divine connection, because God knows who has the experiences, knowledge and giftings that each of us needs to "birth" us into our destiny. He also chooses individuals whom he can trust to carry out his will to the end in spite of the kick-back.

Through fasting, God showed me that selfishness and being self-consumed, can facilitate an anti-God environment. So when God wants to create unity and love in our environment, we can prove to be antagonistic to it because we are self-consumed. We react not discerning that we are not working along with God in building what He wants to build. That is why I believe the prayer says, "Thy kingdom come, and thy will be done". We put aside our desires to hear and see what God is doing so that we can work along with Him; not Him doing what we want.

When the person who is hearing from God, and is working along with Him meets the person who is self-absorbed, there can be friction and misunderstandings because they are at different levels spiritually, and it spills over into other aspects of the relationship. Another observation I made during the fast was that there was less friction and misunderstandings, because I became less absorbed with self and was more considering God and others. I also trusted God more in terms of timing for things to happen. God will align it to be so and it will happen in His perfect timing, I don't need to act up about it, or become frustrated with flesh and blood, because God is the one who has the divine order over when things happen. Conversations became effortless, and flowed naturally with no friction and disagreements, because somehow the flesh becomes subdued to the Spirit of God, and you seek after peace and the things that God wants. The peace of God also settles your spirit, so that your relationships are impacted by what God is doing in you, and you also see others through God's eyes, which is what I prayed for during the fast as well.

Fasting sensitises us to the Spirit of God and what His will is in a given situation.

The emotion of jealousy, I read once, is something that can exist in every type of relationship, because people want something for themselves and see others receiving it. This can evoke that emotion. Even if God connects your best friend or spouse with someone legitimately, when you are sensitive to the Spirit of God, it will not disturb you in the same way as an ungodly and unhealthy connection. You will discern that the connection is to fulfil the purposes and will of God, in the lives of the persons being connected. Fasting helps to bring down all things that exalt itself against God, and bring them into subjection to God's will.

Fasting can help internal struggles

In addition to helping relationships, fasting can effectively break fleshly struggles in our lives. I find that when I fast, I have the strength to resist sexual temptations which, of course, starts with lust in the mind. When fasting was lacking in my life, the slightest lustful thought led to other actions easily. But when fasting became a discipline, I found that there was no desire to engage in sinful activities, not even a thought because I didn't want to spoil the closeness I felt with the Lord, nor reverse the changes God started to effect in my life since the fasting started.

Another impact I realised was that with all the crime and violence happening in our nation, I experienced some level of fear, but since the fasting I realised my faith in the protection of God broke forth, and I believe that if purpose is on my life, He will preserve, protect and hide me from mine enemies and the enemy of my soul. I find I am also praying with faith, as I also immerse in the Word of God, because faith comes as I read the Word through the fast.

I struggled with discontentment, which is not being happy in the situation I found myself in, and always searching for better or for change the minute I became discontent. I was discontent with my current state in life and singleness. Since the fast, I find I can agree with what Paul said "In whatever state I am I learn to be content". The Lord gave me a heart that appreciates my current state and seeks to fulfil the purpose in it, while I aspire after my goals in life. He showed me that being married won't make me happy and changing your job won't either cause if you don't find that you get what you desired you will change your situation and still be unhappy. People wait for an event to happen before they are happy, but the truth is if you don't have the joy already, you won't have it when you are dissatisfied. You will be the kind of person that is always longing for something more to make you happy. Jesus is becoming the centre of my joy, so even when I don't find all my material and emotional needs are met, I won't be hurt and disappointed, but turn to Him for comfort. Once I am in the will of the Lord that is where I find my peace, knowing I am where God wants me to be.

A biological sister who is also
a friend – what a gift!

CHAPTER SIX

FRIENDS: IRREFUTABLE GIFTS

*"At times our own light goes out and is
rekindled by a spark from another person.
Each of us has cause to think with deep
gratitude of those who have lighted the flame
within us."*
-- Albert Schweitzer

I could not write a book of this nature without mentioning the little "rocks" that have made my life so meaningful. I truly don't know how I would have made it this far, and have such a rich life without some persons, male and female, who have stood the test of time, been through thick-and-thin with me, taken some of the "blows" of life meant for me, and were able to exult with me in my victories. These are called friends! What each of us needs. Relationships outside of our family but feels like family. In some cases, friends come closer to you than family, knowing your ins and outs, ups and downs, where you have made it, and where you have lost it. They hold secrets that they take to the grave. But this is never a one-way street. In order to have great friends, one has also to prove oneself friendly. What are some characteristics that are needed to be such a friend to others, and be able to attract this rich and true gift from others, called friendship?

F- FAITHFULNESS - this is that indomitable ability to stick to someone, not in an emotionally dependent unhealthy manner, but in times when the crowd would move away. These might be times of embarrassment, financial loss, marital/family breakup, legal battles, and grief. It is a type of consistency when you are going through challenging times, and others are too busy to share the burden and even to care. There is a loyalty that money can't buy and as far as is possible, they are there to support you verbally or otherwise in your endeavours, helping you to build your dreams. What makes it a real-ationship is when this is mutually done. It is not one always on the giving end while the other is always receiving.

As I write, I have many faithful friends, but I will choose to write about the longest friend, my friend from High School

R- REAL - it is having that ability to be transparent, revealing who we really are. The truth is I don't know any other way that a deep friendship can develop between one or two persons, who operate on a superficial level. I have wondered how two persons can speak of being very close and having a tight relationship, yet they hide true feelings and opinions from each other. They relate on one level, e.g. always telling jokes but when their backs are turned, the sorrow of their heart appears. This word real also suggests a level of honesty, that although we might not want to expose things that are deep in our hearts with acquaintances, we are willing to do so with our friends.

I- INTEGRITY - this too speaks of honesty but in this context I want to emphasize truthfulness, even if it means being misunderstood. A good friend will tell his/her friend where he/she is going wrong. It is not usually an easy step to take. and could make the waters of the friendship a bit muddy for a time, but out of love and honour for that friend, you will do it. Friendships cannot be based on selfishness or self-preservation. It is usually thinking about the welfare of the other person.

E- EMERGENCY - Ecclesiastes 4:10 ESV says,

"For if they fall, one will lift up his fellow. But woe to him who is alone when he falls and has not another to lift him up!" A true friend is such a person. This person seeks to lift you up when you are down and will see the urgency in doing so ASAP. He/She does not need to take a lot of time to mull over it. If there is an emergency with you or even with your loved one, a true friend will act appropriately to assist in that need.

N- NON-JUDGEMENTAL - This speaks of a friend's ability to listen to and observe his/her friend's failings without becoming judge and jury in the case. Again, this is not suggesting that a friend condones wrong, because it is a friend who is now guilty. It is not suggesting either that he/she turns a blind eye on evil, especially since it is done by a friend. A non-judgmental attitude is one that, having accepted that another has done wrong, does not criticize and keep finding or harping on the faults of the other. Their evaluation of their friend's action is not based on their own biases or opinions, but they can look objectively yet graciously at the fault, and help their faltering friend to change their wrong course of behaviour.

D- DEPENDABLE - We recently had a birthday party for my husband. This was one word that kept coming up as his friends and co-workers were toasting him. They were describing a quality observed and experienced, which made them feel like they could go to bed in peace knowing that my husband was going to do his part as promised. I could sit there nodding, because I too found him to be very dependable. He is a true friend. A true friend is truly reliable, and you can have confidence in that person. They are trustworthy, faithful, and stable.

My childhood and current friend, Sharon Nash has decided to make a contribution to this chapter. She speaks from the heart of a friendship that we have shared since we were both teenagers.

Testimony of my Lifetime Friend – Shar

Maria – A True Friend

"You know that Maria Vassell (maiden name) turn Christian?" My teenage ears pricked up. Could it be true that the same Maria that was dancing on the TV programme "Where

it's At"; this apparently anything but religious Maria Vassell is now really a Christian? I needed to investigate this phenomenon. That I did and was pleasantly surprised that this was indeed the real deal! She not only professed to love our now common Lord Jesus Christ but was passionately living it. Yes!

We not only had a few courses in common, but we also were both student leaders in our high school, and so had opportunity to work together. We began sharing life experiences and looked forward to swapping testimonies of God's goodness. We even pioneered a Student Bible Study Group, where we and a few other Christian girls took turns leading the weekly after school Friday meeting. She was now my bona fide friend. We talked about everything and encouraged the best in and for each other. Laughter and hilarious dramatized storytelling was a regular feature of our shared lives. The highlight of our times together however, was our praying in agreement. It was so exciting to see God answer our prayers, and we grew in faith as we spurred each other on to persist in intercession when the answers were long in coming. Our friendship was definitely a place where God was, and still is real and present.

Our friendship was watered by our regular times of connection which continued for decades. I had no doubt that she respected me and loved me. The feeling was mutual. God had given us to each other and His gift was good. We were ourselves with each other. Honesty is so freeing, and this liberty made our friendship soar. I was inspired by how confessional my friend was and still is. Her courage to face the truth about herself is contagious. It also makes it easy to give her negative feedback, which is usually a challenging task for me. But not with Maria, who only wants to please our God and be the best Maria she can be.

How can you not flourish in a friendship when that friend is tender when you are vulnerable; is excited when you succeed; is forgiving when you offend; is patient when you forget; and accepting when you are disappointing; loving when you are unlovable; safe when you are scared, confused and mixed up; whose prayers carry you when you can't walk another step? This is indeed God watering his precious exotic flowers with gentle rain. We grow together, though so different, but with united vision and touching souls.

Maria has been present for me even when we have lived in different countries with no internet or cell phones. She is the sure face in the crowd at every major life celebration, and the hand holding mine at every time of mourning. She has actively loved my family members and they love her. I love hers and they celebrate what we have.

We both have other good friends that we cherish and speak of with each other. There is no room for envy, jealousy or comparisons, for we both know the uniqueness of what we share in our relationship. There is no fear in mature love. Though there is truth speaking, there is no judgment. Authentic, genuine, precious is my friend Maria. God has done all things well, and decades later I am still thanking Him.

-Shar-

But I say unto you
which hear,
Love your enemies, do
good to them which
hate you
Luke 6:27

CHAPTER SEVEN

DEALING WITH MY ENEMIES

"I know from personal experience how damaging it can be to live with bitterness and unforgiveness. I like to say it's like taking poison and hoping your enemy will die. And it really is that harmful to us to live this way." -- Joyce Meyer

I grew up loving people as a small child. There was no one that I did not like. That was positive but at the same time it had a negative effect on my life. It meant that I was very trusting including of males. I was not afraid of the male specie because I grew up with three older brothers and they had friends who visited our home. The truth is, I felt secure around males. I was a little tomboy in some ways, as I got accustomed to playing the games like cricket and football which were seen to be "masculine" games at that time.

I remember traveling on the public transportation, a big bus which was packed up with people and no seats remaining. A man invited me to sit on his lap and I did. I was glad to sit and nothing wrong happened. A woman called out to me when I was leaving the bus and said to me, "Little girl, you must never sit in a strange man's lap". Out of respect I responded, "Yes Mam". I was puzzled. Why did she say that and this stranger was kind to me, I was thinking. It was not long after that I discovered that not only strangers, but sometimes neighbours who were trusted by my own family, were seeking to take advantage of me sexually.

My love/liking of all persons made me vulnerable to emotional pain, when different ones of them tried to hurt me – by accusing me falsely; by physically harming me, or by rejecting me for no apparent reason. I began to learn that not everyone was intrinsically trustworthy, and not everyone was protective of children. The world became a frightening place, and I was afraid to fight back. I was not really taught how to or who to turn to when others tried to hurt me. The truth is my mother was always a "turn the other cheek" and do not repay evil with evil. When I became a teenager, I realized that there was no one to defend me, so I had to learn to defend myself. I still was not a fighter physically, but my mouth became my weapon and I became feisty. I also noted how easily people hurt others and I no longer liked people en mass in the same way as I did before. I learnt that people can become your enemies whether you like it or not.

Malice entered my heart. I no longer wanted to relate to my friends who betrayed me. I stopped talking to them. I even began resenting my own mother, because I saw her as too forgiving of others who were mistreating her or any of her children. I now had persons in my life who I considered to be enemies. I also realized that I too was treated as an enemy by some persons.

Who is an **enemy**? An enemy is:

- a person who feels hatred for, fosters harmful designs against, or engages in antagonistic activities against another; an adversary or opponent.

- an armed foe; an opposing military force:

- a hostile nation or state.

[https://www.dictionary.com/browse/enemy]

How Do People Become Our Enemies?

In the same way that people become friends by exhibiting certain characteristics, so do enemies by exhibiting the opposite characteristics.

The point is that enemies themselves might have far more troubles than you, and because they don't know you really, it is easy for them to be destructively critical, to forego concern, and easily duck, turn, or hide from being discovered as incompetent to understand you, judge you, or comment on the issues at hand.

It's also possible for your enemies to be mature people, and even good people, but ones who don't like you and whom you don't like in return.

What matters to your welfare is that they are neither a constructive critic, nor an advocate. They only have destructive criticism for you, and if asked, would actually advocate against you rather than keep the neutrality of an old time journalist. [https://www.psychologytoday.com]

I would like to use the acronym E.N.E.M.Y. to illustrate some general characteristics of an enemy.

E- EVILDOER - this refers to those who are **troublemakers** in our lives – they make trouble for us, sometimes without any logical explanation. These are persons who cause difficulties, distress, worry to you usually on more than one occasion, but it does not need to be continuous harassment. A troublemaker can stir up trouble or strife in, for example, a family. When this is done, one lie for example, can lead to the destruction of healthy families.

As I write, I can think about this happening in marriages leading to trust being broken and relationships struggling to recover from deep hurt and disappointment, just because of someone's tongue that meant to do evil to one or both individuals. It really is sad to see how quick persons are to believe a lie. Therefore, it becomes easier for enemies to concoct their worse weaponry in their arsenal.

N - NEGATIVE – these are persons who in words, thoughts and/or behaviour are unbalanced and unhealthy in their **perspective**. They can spoil and cause even those with strong faith and positive outlooks on life to begin to doubt themselves and others. They are not helpful to us especially if they are

206

intentionally seeking to get us to change our minds about something or someone who is or has a positive influence in our lives. Have you ever been excited about doing a project, and having done your research you are convinced that it could succeed but up comes Miss/Mr Negative. He/She can convince you/others that you are being stupid; you are acting selfishly and seeking some personal glory; if it has failed before, who do you think that you are that will make it work this time? This is not to say that constructive criticism, or plausible questioning of persons who really want to know and understand what you/they are getting into, are enemies. No. We do need persons like these within families and on committees. Enemies are usually bitter on the inside and that bitterness covers their perspectives. They filter what others say through bitterness and negativity. They are like the miserable seeking to make others miserable along with them, and won't stop until they find disciples.

E - ENIGMATIC - this speaks of persons who relate to us but are always a **problem** and a **puzzle** to us. They tend to operate mystically with the end-result of confusing others. They don't want to be friendly but to have a high wall of defense that keeps others far from them, and in some way this brings them personal pleasure and allows them to have an advantage over others. The more persons try to get close and to "scale" their psychological walls, the more they may be attacked by this person as a warning to keep their distance and not to seek to figure them out. They are antagonistic – always opposing and even hostile without an explanation. Some persons will remain distant with such a person since we often fear what we don't understand, and perceive as possibly being harmful to us. This distance is at times advisable since this strange behaviour is engaged in, while they are conspiring and concocting some evil plot to bring someone down, or to get others out of the race of life. By the time their evil plan rolls out, the victim is in shock. They had seen the strange behaviour, but could not put their finger on what was going on within the perpetrator.

M- MALICIOUS - persons who are mean-spirited, hurtful, malevolent, having wicked intentions towards others. This is not just that others may feel hurt or offended by their words and actions, but those who are malicious, their **motive** is to cause hurt and pain. They speak or act intentionally to sabotage someone else, to destroy someone's reputation; they are heartless or ruthless because their intention is to harm others.

Sometimes persons are malicious out of envy or jealousy. They want what or who you have. Since they cannot successfully have this, they can become consumed by hate. If there is a prize in a contest, and it is likely that someone is already ahead for that prize, a malicious person will seek to trip them up; spoil their chances of winning in some way. This is not about being competitive; it's about being diabolical in the way that they compete.

What's even worse for me is to observe how, even adults, can maliciously hurt children. It's as if other people's children do not count and should not get ahead in life. Not only would they not lift a finger to help another person's child, but would teach their own children how to step on others to get ahead, not caring who gets hurt or crushed under their weight.

Y- YEARNING FOR STRIFE - this speaks of persons who are highly offensive**,** disgusting**, and** revolting. They are neither comfortable, or at peace unless they are **at odds** with someone. This could be one particular person, e.g. a spouse, child, in-law or everyone with whom they come into contact. I never knew this was possible until I had to relate closely to someone who obviously wanted strife. No matter what I did to avoid an argument, I would be backed into a corner and gored by abusive words, until I gave some response. The individual seemed satisfied when the two tangoed. One day I decided I was not going to fall into this trap. When the person started arguing and howling at me, I stood firm. I decided it takes two hands to clap and I did not answer. The person's response was "So you're not answering; you're not answering?!" This question was repeated several times and the person looked more and more deflated as I kept quiet and did not join in their "game". Prior to this, there was an aspect of animation when they were able to pull others out, and get them to be involved in an argument with them.

When this person came howling at me, I did see the person as an enemy. Why? I could see in their eyes that they were not in my corner; they were seeing me as a threat; they moved closer to me to harm me; they lacked peace and were not comfortable seeing persons being peaceful. This revelation that someone could thrive on strife made me realize as the sayings go, misery finds company and hurting people hurt others. A person's pain can set them up to be an enemy to others, and can repel the very ones that could help them to deal with this pain.

How to Deal With Our Enemies

o **Face the Facts**. If you know why they are resentful towards you, and especially if you know that they were offended by something that you did, it is time to apologize. Even if you did not intend to offend, the fact that whatever was said or done to them was offensive. To reopen a door, you could communicate that your motive was not to be in any way malicious so you regret the fact that they were offended. If it was the truth that was told, you would not apologize for the truth but perhaps the medium by which it was conveyed.

If you are the offended party, face up to the hurt felt. Before confrontation however, you may need to analyze the situation, and be as objective as you can in your assessment of it. Is this person seeking to be malicious and devious, an enemy? Or is it a one-off situation that with a sit-down chat with them, the matter could be resolved? After your objective evaluation, consider the next step(s) and ask: If the person was being malicious, should I approach this person if they could further harm me? Would it be better to have a mutually respected person be present when handling the matter? Or, this mediator speaks with the person on your behalf before any face-to-face confrontation? When dealing with an enemy, it is always good to have a "battle plan"; some kind of strategy having studied with whom and with what you are dealing.

o **Face Your Fears.** What do you fear most about someone who has set themself up as your enemy? Usually that in some way they will be able to access you, someone you love or something you value. Having this open door, they will do harm. When dealing with an enemy, these fears are real. If for example, whenever you speak to someone who is obviously not in your corner, and they twist whatever you say, add what they wish, in order to make others see you as an enemy, fear of such a person is real. If you have such a fear, face up to it and the reasons for it. Fear however brings torment.

18 There is no fear in love. But perfect love drives out fear, because fear has to do with punishment. The one who fears is not made perfect in love. 19 We love because he first loved us.
(1John 4:18-19)

The one you fear can have power over you through this fear. Taking control of this fear is key. Learning to love even our enemies is powerful. If your enemy was seeking to intimidate you through fear-tactics and you stand in the place of love, they end up confused. Loving our enemies, apart from being a command from God (Luke 6:27-36), is also a choice. Those who have made this choice have discovered that they are in a better place having done so, than when they were resentful and revengeful. Eyeballing our enemy with love in our hearts for them in spite of their wickedness, can "melt" their hearts because this was not what they expected nor bargained for.

o **Face Your Alternatives.** Some important decisions need to be made here. Do I respond in like manner? Do I enter a tit-for-tat game? Do I walk away from relating to such a person? Do I just avoid them entirely or relate to them only on a need-to basis? Some alternatives are not easy choices, especially if you are "forced" to be in a living situation, or a working environment with such a person.

o **Face Yourself**. Oftentimes, it is our enemies that expose the weaknesses in us that we need to own and change. If you find yourself using foul language because of someone who is being nasty to you, it is not that person who made you do it. It is time to face up to what is within us. That foul language came from somewhere. Perhaps you learnt some wrong responses to aggravation.

212

CHAPTER EIGHT

GOD GAVE US FAMILY

"It is Jesus that The Proverbs 31 Lady seeks when she dreams of happiness; He is waiting for her when nothing else she finds satisfies her; He is the beauty to which she is so attracted to; it is He who provoked her with that thirst for fullness that will not let her settle for compromise; it is He who urges her to shed the masks of a false life; it is He who reads in her heart her most genuine choices, the choices that others try to suppress." -- Mary Maina

It is amazing what having a family, especially a healthy family life, does to us as individuals. No matter how successful or powerful a person feels, this thing called family real-ationships really makes a difference, if there are those with blood connections, or even adoptive and fostering connections, with whom we can share ourselves and our successes. If there is a place that we can be made for good or bent and broken and in need of fixing as we go through life, it is within the family.

Of all our social institutions, the family is perhaps the one with which we are most familiar. As we proceed through our lives, our experiences within the family give rise to some of our strongest and most intense feelings. Within the family context lies a paradox, however: although most of us hope for love and support within the family -- a haven in a heartless world, so to speak -- the family can also be a place of violence and abuse.

--MARILYN POOLE, Family: Changing Families, Changing Times [Read more at http://www.notable-quotes.com/f/family_quotes.]

As I was beginning this chapter, I had taken time out of my busy schedule to spend some days overseas with my Mom. She was recuperating in a Nursing Home before the hospital released her to go home. As I walked in and saw my Mom for the first time since she was taken to the hospital, I was assailed by a mass of emotions. Initially, for the first time in my life, she did not recognize me, and I was referred to by two nieces names until she finally got it with some prodding by my brother. I felt better the following day when in front of the speech therapist she was able to say my name (using my maiden name) which her long-term memory would be more aware of.

The first time however as I went to see her, upon arrival and seeing her in a wheelchair, looking disconnected and in the midst of strangers, I swallowed hard. Then it was the process of getting her to recognize her only daughter, while her eyes were shifting all over. As I moved in close to her and said "Mom", resting my head against hers, she just let her head lay there. "You are missing home, aren't you?" "Um uh" she responded and her eyes watered. I realized this was hard for her, and she was feeling disoriented being moved from a hospital to a Nursing Home, as lovely and sparklingly clean as it was. She was outside of her 'space' and comfort zone. The words coming from her sounded delusional and interestingly enough, she was calling a name of someone who was deceased over three decades, and she was speaking of having the fire on the stove. She had not been close to a stove for nearly ten years.

When I arrived at her home later that evening, although I had just left her at the Home, I missed our usual first greeting, "Mother Dear" and her customary response, "Wait, Maria? That's you!" I felt a gulf in my stomach as I faced the reality that she was not going to be in her room, and perhaps for the days that I would be in Connecticut. Frankly, I was missing her. As siblings, we spoke about preparing ourselves and always having to face that reality that not many want to face – the inevitable inescapable certainty that one day your parent will die. As we spoke, I could see the expression on the younger of my brothers, Joshua, who for the first time, had several months by her side, serving her. He had expressed when she initially went in the hospital, that he felt sad leaving her in the hospital, since they were one moment doing fine and in the short time that he moved outside, something went wrong. The ambulance was being called because she was not very responsive.

When I returned to the Home the next day, she was looking brighter. She even ate a small cup of ice-cream and fed herself, something that we were accustomed to seeing her do. My Mom has lived for nine decades. By God's grace she is able to go to the bathroom by herself, and consume a meal without anyone's help. I was in the physical therapy room where the therapists were working with her to get strong. I looked at the "state of the art" machines with all the attachments, and I was grateful that she could access this service, and the gentleness of the therapists. She was riding a 'bike' using only rotating hand movements and then with the legs. I thanked the Lord that she was an easy patient. I was trusting that she would get out of there fast, notwithstanding the pleasant environment. No matter where you go, even to the best hotels, there is no place like home, being with ones treasured family and operating in one's comfort zone.

The night before was an emotional night as I cried out to God for her healing. The following day was the last day of visiting with my Mom before I left for another state, and finally to head home to my nuclear family in Jamaica. When I left the Home, she was as restless as she was the night before. I had only just begun to learn about the stages and faces of dementia. My Mom was hardly recognizing people around her, including me. This happened on the final day. She could tell you her daughter's name is Maria, but when I said, "This is Maria", she would look at me strangely and it was obvious that there was no recognition in her eyes. I recalled at that time, a preacher at church telling us how painful it was that his own mother was not recognizing him. We could feel his pain as he related this within his message. While I listened to him, knowing that my mother too was way up in age, I wondered how I would feel and how I would cope. It was now staring me in the face. I was sitting beside her as she was dozing in and out, but she did not seem to be aware that someone was beside her. Even when her eyes were wide open, she was speaking to herself, of things happening in the past without an awareness of the present. How does one transition from a daughter to a "stranger"? There is no easy answer. This was now the reality of our relationship and I could not hide from it! My thought at the time was, *"When I leave in a few hours' time, I don't know what will happen, but I truly place her in God's hands."*

As I was about to leave, a Christian nurse walked into the room, and while conversing with her about the goodness of God, she began relating about His work in her life. She remarked that some of the patients look at her and know there is something different about her. They ask her to pray and some get healed. After sharing her testimony with me, I had the assurance that God had His people around who He had assigned to take care of her. Before she left, she laid her hand on Mom's bed and prayed for God to cover her as she sleeps. She also prayed a prayer of protection over her. Wow. As I listened, I marveled at the wisdom of God. How many times have I been in a similar situation, praying for others? When my Mom needed it, He sent medical "angels". Although concerned, I felt at peace about returning home.

I truly feel close to my Mom now and we have been friends. I say now because it was not always so. I never felt close to her until I was an adult! This statement alone would begin to conjure up some questions in your mind. A child not feeling close to her mother! What could have led to all of this?

I was not born in an ideal relationship. Approximately six months after I was born, by my mother's recollection, she and my father no longer had a relationship. At that point, my Mom was affected by their break-up and withdrew emotionally in her attempt to cope. Getting to know who my Mom really was in my adult life, I realized that she would not have knowingly withdrawn from me, but in effect this is what happened as she dealt with her own pain. I had always wondered why I was so insecure in relationships in my early years of life. Jealousy and possessiveness seem to have characterized my young friendships. The discovery of the root cause came by way of revelation, as the Lord ministered to a group of us who were finding it difficult praying for our fathers. That was the night, in an all-night prayer meeting, that a spirit of rejection was rebuked and broken from my life. Since that time, I had a fairly easy task to change the various insecurities. I was now free to change.

It was a process getting to know and bond with my Mom at that stage of life. I was not accustomed to spending time at home with her. I was so estranged from her, that even if she was not feeling well, I would go out anyway. I did not spend public holidays with family. Whenever I could, I sought to spend weekends away from home. I had always gone out with friends and did not come back home until dark, and sometimes very late. Relationships outside of the home, for various reasons, were more exciting to me than being alone at home, which happened in earlier years when my brothers would be gone checking out their own friends. My Mom, being the sole breadwinner, had to work from 12:00 midday until night. That was another reason that our bond was not strong. In the mornings I would be rushing out to school. Back home from school, Mom would be at work. When she arrived home, sometimes at 10p.m., I would have already been asleep. So what about weekends? That was time for house-cleaning, washing and ironing of clothes for the next week, etc. The kitchen would have been the next place for us to relate. As a child and daughter, I desired to be in the kitchen with my Mom. This was not convenient. Being a poor family, we shared an outside kitchen with another tenant. This was a very small space. It was even too small for my Mom and the other tenant to move around easily. So, I was not able to join her in the kitchen.

I became more estranged from her when an incident of abuse happened in my life. I grew up in the ghetto (inner-city community). One day when I was around 9 years old, I was going to a small grocery shop. I saw one of my friends from the neighbourhood. I stopped her, trying to convince her to turn back and accompany me to the shop. I held one arm and was pulling her in my direction. A small bag of groceries fell from the other hand. I was bending to take it up, when she was complaining that I boxed it out of her hand. As I was bending, two adults who were standing nearby told me not to pick it up, because I did not do what I was being accused of. I was in conflict; wanting to pick up the bag but wanting also to obey the adults. My friend picked up the bag, walked off, and threatened to go to her grandmother to make a complaint. I went to the shop and walked home slowly as I was feeling badly about what happened. I had to pass my friend's gate when going home. As I approached, I saw a large crowd at her gate, and heard a commotion going on. I wondered what it was. As I got closer, her grandmother burst out of the crowd, grabbed me, and began hitting me several times (a few punches too), in the midst of the crowd which was a mix of adults and children. In shock, embarrassment and pain I went home. My Mom was at work and no one was there to console me. I went under my bed and stayed there until evening. No one knowing where I was or what happened.

When my mother came home, she was angry with me! The lady after physically abusing me had also complained to my mother. My Mom rebuked me for what I did (the girl's story). I withdrew. I was disappointed. Instead of my Mom defending me, I thought, she is siding with someone who beat up her child?! It was more than disappoint*ment. I resented her from that day onwards. The resentment in me was broken when I became a Christian teenager and decided to speak the truth to her.* It came out more in the form of an accusation. I accused her of not standing up for me on that occasion, when I was beaten up by the elderly lady. My mother looked at me in shock. "She did what?" she asked. I told her then what happened and that she came home rebuking me. "I did not know that this happened," she replied. "No one told me this. I was told that you boxed something that belonged to her from her grand-daughter's hand, and refused to pick it up. Had I known that she beat you up, it would not have stopped there!" That day I realized that she would have defended me if she knew. I dropped the resentment and began looking at her differently.

I became a Christian at fifteen years old. This is when the tables began turning in every aspect of life. This was when the Scriptures began speaking to my heart about the importance of honouring your parents. The young lady, Jackie, who led me to the Lord and discipled me as a young Christian, was the one who encouraged me to cultivate a relationship with my mother. It was hard at first, but I was determined to obey the Word of God. After a few years, my mother became a Christian herself. Now we were "sisters" and this helped as we spoke a lot together about Church. I attended her Church for her baptism. She had to give a testimony to the fact that she was now a believer in Jesus Christ. When my quiet mother began her testimony, I was stunned. I was thinking, "Do I know this woman?" She spoke with boldness – such confidence about her Lord and what He was already doing for her. I have often said to others that after I became a Christian, my Mom must have said, "There must be a God! Who could rein in my daughter and settle her but Him! I must serve Him."

As we grew closer, a wakeup call came later. We were stepping up into a high vehicle one afternoon on our way to an event. I allowed my mother to step up before me and I am glad I did because she began to fall backwards. I had contrasting emotions as we headed to the event. I was happy that she did not fall but also annoyed at her. I sat in the vehicle trying to analyze my feelings. Why was I so annoyed – maybe even angry? Then I heard a still small voice say: "You are accustomed to your Mom taking care of you; it is your time to take care of her now." Wow. The negative feeling left. An overwhelming peace came over me and from that day forward, the tables switched. I wanted to take care of her and look out for her needs. When she migrated, as much as possible I traveled to see her to connect with her. At those times, we went to Prayer Conferences together, prayed together, discussed family matters, and even planned for the future. Things that we were unable to do before God intervened in both of our lives.

I continue to write from her health facility where she is receiving different therapies. I am now slowly facing the realities that many families have had to face. Unless God miraculously intervenes, the delusions may continue; she might not walk fully on her own as she was doing up to three weeks ago. Some have wondered if it was the side-effects of the medication treating an infection. No one knows. The staff still thinks she is doing very well for her age. We the family, have to keep reminding ourselves that she is past 90 years old. How does one prepare oneself for the inevitable – death of an elderly parent? This subject I will deal with at the end of this chapter.

Why Do We Need a Family?

Family was God's idea. He knew that we needed, from the moment we came on the earth, nourishment, nurture, protection and persons around us to fill our emotional tanks.

➢ **Nourishment.** It is the family, not a Government that a child should look to for proper nutrition. In the unusual cases, the Government has to pick up the slack for the orphans and those children whose parents are incapable of responsibly managing their home affairs.

➢ **Nurture.** When I think of nurture, I think of the tender care of the young, watching over them spiritually, emotionally and physically. Helping them to meet each area of need in an age-appropriate manner. One thing that is strongly needed while children are growing up is support and encouragement. This is oftentimes what makes a big difference between the children who do well in school and pursue their God-given talents and giftings.

➢ **Protection**. To guard, shield, secure and defend, are important responsibilities that two adults who decide to bring a child into the world, have to be prepared for. One of the worst experiences of a child is to be looking to trusted adults, especially parents and other family members for security, and instead they receive abuse or are left exposed for others to abuse them. That I know by firsthand experience. This book is about real-ationships, and therefore unveiling the truth about one's experiences in relationships so that others may be helped. In the years of my earlier childhood, while my mother was at work, I experienced various types of abuse. These took place within the family, including extended family and within the community. I thank the Lord that sexual abuse was not a part of my family, if one is not counting an older family member engaging in illicit sexual dance moves in front of a small child, over and over, to the entertainment of adult neighbours. Now, doing the math, I realized that youth was only a few years older than I was, but very mature for his age. The adults around encouraged his behaviour and cheered him on. I remember looking on in disgust and thinking to myself, "that is so lewd".

Within the family, the type of physical abuse, not by my mother, maybe was not considered abuse, but when there are permanent scars left on your body, it had to be abuse. The truth is, when I was growing up and within the community I grew up, physical abuse seemed to be the norm, including spousal abuse. Child abuse of all types was commonplace. Now with the media, including social media being more vocal, there is more exposure.

Two experiences that had left an indelible mark on my psyche, was when two children under the age of nine years old were raped, one by a father and the other by a step-father. Mine was the unfortunate experience of visiting that friend and seeing her crying, crouched in the corner outside her house and revealing to me, another child, that her step-father did something bad to her! She could hardly speak but managed to tell me what he did. She was in pain and left alone to bear that pain. As a child I did not know what to do except encouraging her to tell her mother. I was disturbed and angry at what was done to my friend. When we met up again, we did not discuss it. Soon after, they moved away and I wondered what happened to her, and whether or not that step-father was still around. In my case, molestation came from all around, except in my home. Being left alone so often, there were persons around, including neighbours, who knew that you were without protection and swooped down on me, some pretending to be caring adults. One even told others when I was around that I was his "daughter". Although very young, I wondered, would he be making attempts at his own daughter in this way, and would he be okay with it if an adult male was doing that to his daughter? At the onset of puberty, I began to develop a tough crust and became very feisty to these men, so they did not try to approach me.

What A Family Should Do When There is Abuse

o The possibility of exposure to abuse should not be in the child's life in the first place. Children should be warned and guided into how to conduct themselves, especially when they sense that there is some threat / an adult, be it stranger, family or friend, wants to pass certain boundaries with them. They should be told who to report it to and given the assurance that the matter will be acted upon.

o The child must be assured that the parents are there to protect him/her even if the perpetrator threatens to harm them or their loved ones. Children who suffered abuse, whenever a threat is issued, now feel that they have to protect their family. They are now carrying two loads: the one of the abuse and the other, the burden of protecting their family. It is very important that children believe and understand that safety is with their parents, and it's their parents' duty to protect them; not the other way around. They are already feeling unsafe because of the perpetrator. They must now feel and know that their parent/guardian will do all within their power, even if it means, changing their habitation, in order to protect them.

o The adult(s) to whom the abuse is reported should now act in the child's interest even if this means separation of the child/family from the abuser. Justice must always be seen to be done by the victim, who will now be encouraged not to hide wrongdoing.

o In some cases, the police / other agents may have to be called in. The child must be constantly assured that he/she is not a troublemaker. They must be shielded as much as possible from the perpetrator attempting to use manipulative or threatening tactics to silence them, or to get them to change the truth. The child might naturally feel guilty if there is an arrest, therefore the adult members need to assure him/her that they did the correct thing, to report the incident.

o Counselling might be needed to assist the child in overcoming any trauma associated with the abuse. Emotional healing of the child must be a priority. These things don't usually go away by adults telling the child to just forget about the incident(s). The adults protecting the child may need counselling too to deal with anger management and feelings of reprisal. The perpetrator will definitely need professional help. In all the proceedings, it must always be uppermost in the adults' minds, that this is a tough experience for the child-victim. Just having to recall the incident of abuse, and then having to voice is to the relevant persons including law-enforcement officers could perpetuate the trauma. The child might even seem resistant to reveal it but keep in mind that for that child, they would like to believe that they just woke up out of a nightmare, and their reality is different.

This type of trauma is not one that any parent/guardian wishes to face, but it is not one that cannot be overcome if the family gets together and strategizes how best to bring healing, first to the child and to all those around who are negatively affected.

Preparing for the Death of a Family Member

While visiting my Mom and siblings in Connecticut, we had to prepare ourselves just in case. My brother Danny, her caretaker, and I discussed how we would go about doing her funeral, etc. I had to go in a clinical mode. Speaking in matter-of-fact language what you would rather avoid ,yet knowing that we have to face that reality. We did not include my other brother because he thought we were being negative. I realized that he was not at the same place to deal with it. He was just missing her and wanting her back home. My mother bounced back and is doing well but it was not the same for my Dad.

Death of My Father

In March 2019, I had this sense of urgency to go to visit my father overseas. He was in the hospital and was sending "I love you" messages to all his children, as if saying goodbye to us. Two of my sisters and I decided to travel overseas to visit with him. Another sister who lives within his country but was about 12 hours away, flying time, joined us. The four of us came and left at different times. Another sister had traveled to be with him for ten days prior to our coming. Others of our siblings attempted to visit but for various reasons, including visa problems, they were unable to. It was heart-breaking for those who really wanted to see him but could not get there in time.

I was with him for four days then he passed. I was somewhat prepared because although he could not speak, he squeezed my hand several times to send us a strong message: "I am prepared to die. Don't hold me back!" I had asked him some questions about his desire to live or die, based on his medical team's advice since he was refusing to take his medication and food. I began to prepare myself, but some family members and friends were not accepting it. When I told them what Dad had communicated by squeezing my hand, I was surprised that he was preparing them from months before he lost his speech. I still felt grief and so did others although we knew that it was coming. Preparation, especially because Dad was honest with us and made practical preparation for his death, softened the blow for me. How then can we prepare for the inevitable? Have a plan in place for it!

a) *Discuss and Arrange Funeral Plans in Advance*

Funeral plans are never easy, especially when you are struggling with the inevitable, but this should be done before the death. Funerals are expensive. The family needs to know how those expenses are going to be covered, e.g. the dying member's life insurance policies, money in the banks or other financial institutions, etc. They will need to know who has power of attorney (who can sign and do other legal transactions in case of death or other impediments). Some of these things, e.g. in the case of my father's insurance, it took weeks after his death for the money to be accessed, so there was the need for money in advance. My father had left his affairs in the hands of an elderly friend who had already worked these things out, prior to his death.

Making the actual arrangements was difficult, and I was glad that my Dad's elderly friend was not left to handle the arrangements alone. It was tough-going but it could have been worse if my Dad had not done some things like:

- *Communicating where he wanted the Church service; where he wanted to be buried; who should participate in the service and what specifically he wanted them to do; that his body not be cremated. Family members, if this information is not being volunteered by the terminally ill relative, you will need to seek ways to get them to discuss this. As you speak among yourselves, there might be a member with whom he mentioned his preferences. Take the time to find out before the death.*

- *Handing over all the relevant papers, including his will to his friend, so when the funeral parlour requested certain documents, there were right there with us. They were the ones taking care of all the legal matters for his Government. Leaving the parlour, having signed the relevant documents, it was off to purchase the plot.*

- *Doing his farewell speeches. As much as it was obvious that many around him did not like him speaking of his death, he made sure to make us aware when it was drawing closer to the time. Each family member had some time alone with him. Those of us who had not seen him, some in years, had flown in to be with him, realizing that these were the closing moments of his life. Each had the opportunity to make their peace if they wished to do so.*

I had gone to visit him preparing myself in case he passed while I was there. It happened that my Dad passed the day before I was scheduled to leave the country. I had to change flight plans and make hotel arrangements to remain there, and to assist in whatever way I could with the funeral arrangements. Anticipating the possibilities is important. If someone is terminally ill, like my Dad was, one has to listen to the health professionals treating him. In our case, his doctor told us the day before he died, that his kidneys were now shutting down. I knew what that meant.

b) *Deal With Your Issues Before Death Takes Place.*

Death can bring out the worst in some relatives. It is during the time of emotional stress and distress on the family, when they choose to create more stress by being negative in their pronouncements; wrongly accusing other members; making unrealistic demands on the family. Their timing is poor. If there are real issues to be dealt with, it should be approached as calmly as possible, especially if it has to be done in the hearing of the terminally ill loved one. They are usually too weak to take on any heavy issues so it is more beneficial to be considerate.

c) ***Know the Significant Persons to Contact When the Death Takes Place.*** *One needs to know this list of persons preferably before the death, beginning with family members, employer(s), heads of organizations with which the person is associated, e.g. their pastor. Other official agencies will need to be contacted so they can, for example, freeze the person's accounts until the authorized person(s) come forward to access it. In a world where there is so much corruption and scamming, family members who are in charge need to keep on the alert in spite of overwhelming grief. It is a sad note, but even some relatives might be opportunists, and take advantage of the family's vulnerability at this time. Some families employ, officially or unofficially, someone who is knowledgeable, experienced and objective, to pilot the events that will take place after the death.*

d) ***Plan in Advance How You are Going to be Supportive After the Death.***

If the terminally ill relative will be leaving behind people who are dependents, each family member could consider how they will offer support, and how they will also receive the support of others. All types of strange and mixed emotions might erupt within individuals, and can affect the family negatively even after the funeral. Family members should decide to keep their bond in spite of anger, resentment, feelings of being left out at some stage of the planning, etc. They can voice their feelings but the "blame game" should be avoided. Adversarial confrontations should be avoided, and if there are deep issues that have to be resolved, it may need the intervention of a professional counsellor, who is gifted with the ability to protect each party as they meander their way through grieving and the healing process.

There are families that have become stronger even after the death of a loved one. Yours can be one of those too.

Don't forget that God understands grief and loss. He is there to comfort and to guide. This is the time to get closer to God too. He will have an open ear to your cries and be attentive to your brokenness.

CHAPTER NINE

SPEAKING OF GOD: MY LOVER, MY FRIEND

"There will always be someone willing to hurt you, put you down, gossip about you, belittle your accomplishments and judge your soul. It is a fact that we all must face. However, if you realize that God is a best friend that stands beside you when others cast stones you will never be afraid, never feel worthless and never feel alone — Shannon L. Alder

I wish that I could say that since I met Jesus as my personal Saviour and Lord at the age of 15, I never felt afraid, worthless or alone. The truth is, in my real-ationship with God, it took me a while to settle down and feel secure, although I was seeking after Him with all of my heart. From as far back as I can remember, I have always loved Jesus. My Sunday School teacher at the time had a lot to do with this, as she related to us the great and marvelous things that God did back in Bible days, and continued to do for His children and the world in general. You could not stop me from going to Sunday School. If I was sick, my mother would not know of it since she would suggest that I not go. However, somehow by the time Sunday School/Church was finished, I would be alright. I did not know that anyone or anything could have turned me off from attending church.

My Childhood Experiences

It was after the Christmas programme. I was about 12 years old. I was chosen to narrate the big Christmas play at Church on Christmas morning. The entire play was miming. Everyone was hoping they would get the only speaking part – narrator of the play. I was elected to be the narrator. Not a surprise to me because my teachers used to comment on my elocution, and I was often chosen to do poetry and other readings at school functions. My getting this part though, stirred up anger in some of the youth and the gossip started. Some very unkind remarks were made and rumours were circulating concerning me. By the time I realised, I had already made many enemies. I was very disappointed. Deeply hurt that I was treated that way and I had not done anyone harm. As a child I could not understand.

I withdrew and stopped going to Church. My life after that took a downward slope. No longer was I going after God but got involved with friends and activities that I should not have at my age – experimenting with smoking, drinking, going to adult movies and parties, etc. My life became lonelier. My home life was disjointed. My schoolwork which was excellent prior to this suffered, causing much frustration in my teachers who knew my potential. Entertainment was now my game. I passed exams but not because I studied hard. After school I would go skating after coming home and changing my uniform. Music...music...music. Dancing...dancing...dancing. I ended up by age 13 as a dancer on a popular television programme. Then came the betrayals – best-friend, boy-friend. There was so much pain in my heart by this time that I often wonder how I carried it. It was the right and ripe time for Jesus to show up in my life. He did when I was in fourth form in High School. At age 15, I was "born again". The experience was like hands lifting a sack of bricks from off my shoulders. I was so light after I surrendered to Jesus. I had now started what would have turned out to be an adventurous journey with Him, that would take me through many blessings but also trials and temptations. This I was determined would be a real-ationship with God. I hated double-standards, and decided from then that I was going to be real (truthful) with Him. I was going to serve Him with my whole heart!

> *"But I beg of you, fear God and worship him honestly and heartily. You've seen how greatly he has worked among you!" [1 Sam 12:24]*

Kidnapped

My first traumatic experience that could have made me give up the faith came when as a sixth former, I was kidnapped and held for about 2 hours near the National Stadium. I was now a Christian for 2 years when this happened. I was threatened and forced to go on a bike by a man who stopped me to ask me for directions. He began to tell me why he was trying to get to that address (to deliver clothes for his children). Suddenly, the man's eyes changed right in front of me. I was startled. He then began to threaten me and ask me for money. He pulled my graduation ring from my finger and would have taken it, except that it could not fit any of his fingers. I only had my bus fare in my wallet, so he threw it back at me. He then ordered me to get on the bike with him and threatened that if I attempt to get anyone's attention, he would shoot me. It was now dusk, and my thinking was that he would have to ride through some built up area. I planned to jump off the bike even if I hurt myself, but I determined that I would not go all the way with him. He surprised me, and turned the bike into some bushes across from the National Stadium. It did not take me long to realize that rape was the motive.

After much dramatics I managed to convince this ugly, at least twice my age stranger, that I was sick in the lower part of my body (STD) and was going to the doctor the next day. This lie he bought into after much questioning, BUT then demanded oral sex. I was in shock and totally humiliated by the crudeness of his language as he demanded this action. A struggle ensued and I resisted with everything within me. The next thing I knew was that I felt wet on my dress. He had ejaculated on the front of my dress.

Although he was not successful in the act, I was traumatized by the ordeal and felt like killing him, when he told me after that he did not have a gun in his bag, as he said he did when he threatened to kill me. I was livid. I wanted to smash his head with a stone. I had to travel home with sperm all over my dress. I went home in a daze and I don't recall the journey home. I must have still been in shock. I remember however, meeting my Mom at the gate but was not close to her then. I told no one at home what happened. I could not stop bathing when I got home. My tears were mixed with the water that did not seem to be able to make me feel clean enough.

I could not reconcile my faith with what just happened and for weeks I struggled. Whenever I heard a bike rumbling pass the bus I was travelling in, I would almost panic. If it was near my stop, I would freeze and not want to get off the bus. I received prayer a few days after, but it was not until God gave a man of God, Col. Mason, one of my spiritual fathers, a severe stomach pain while he was sitting and counselling with me one day. It was when he demanded that I release the information of my trauma, that I finally told the whole story. He prayed and I got my breakthrough. I realized that God was so touched by my pain that he caused another to experience it briefly. Praise God I was healed. I was free. No more chains in my mind. My memory and emotions were healed. Interestingly, not long after, I ended up helping other persons who had similar experiences some years before, but had never talked about it.

Short Stint With a Cult

Two years after I became a Christian and still in sixth form, I met a teacher who was religious, but later found out that she was a part of a cult. Out of curiosity, I visited one of her meetings with her. She was like a mother-sister-friend, so I was curious to attend with her. While there however, the leader asked us to write our name on a piece of paper, so that from it she could tell us about our lives. Immediately I had a check in my spirit – this is wrong. This is an occult practice. No sooner than this thought came, the leader who was sitting at the far end of the table we were all sitting at, shouted at me that I should "stop condemning" what she was doing! How did she know what I was thinking? I was frightened and became scared of her. Everyone else was writing so I wrote my name. She asked me questions that would suggest she was getting knowledge from the "dark world". This was definitely not from God. I later discovered that she was anti-Christ. A popular reggae band, its members, would come to her prior to a show to get her "blessing". She would wrap their turbans for them. Once the cult leader instructed me that when I attend an evangelistic meeting that was being held at the arena, I should say a particular word (this was not an English word). I did not know what I was saying. I knew deep down that all of this was wrong, but fear gripped me. What would she do to me if I should disobey? This went on for about four months when God entered the Art Room at my High School one Saturday when I was the only one who turned up out of about six of us practicing for exams. God warned me to cut my friendship with this teacher (this was the second time). I was under deep conviction and could not hurt my Lord anymore by joining with this anti-Christ spirit. I needed ministry and turned to one of my spiritual fathers with whom I had a real-ationship. I told him everything and he confirmed what God had said to me. It would be dangerous to continue relating to these persons.

When I cut the friendship, the reaction was austere. I had wanted us to be civil with each other but not the other party. Malice was what came back at me. Open malice. It seemed she wanted everyone to know that she had cut me off. It was painful but with the prayers of my close Christian school friends, I came through victoriously. I was delivered from the fear. This was not a small fear. If I was standing on the road and saw the leader's car coming, I felt as if I was going to have a heart-attack! I needed God's intervention to get rid of it and God did deliver. Mine was a short stint with a cult, but if you ever have to deal with someone who is trying to get free from a cult, this fear is real.

I was selected to be the Valedictorian at my Graduation from seminary. I was led to speak on the topic, FAITHFULNESS REGARDLESS. I was 23 years old and addressed the graduates on walking faithfully before God, in spite of what we would face after leaving bible school. I felt like this was something God was asking of me too. I could not have guessed at that time how this would have been tested in my lifetime.

Brokenhearted

I had an experience that I have to be real about. At 19 years old, I was praying about a partner for life. There was someone who I had liked at the time and in the midst of praying, the Lord spoke to me and assured me that He was going to provide a tremendous husband for me and would fill my life with joy. As a youth and not having much experience, I assumed that the person who I was attracted to and praying about at the time, had to be such a person, because he was the best single male I had known up to that time. We went out once. We spoke on the phone. He spoke to one of our spiritual leaders, who gave him some words of wisdom about taking care of some other business before embarking on another relationship. The big test came for me when in college, they wanted to choose someone to be an exchange student with another college in the USA. I was encouraged by many of my fellow seminarians to apply. I hesitated...I resisted...I closed the door. The reason is that I was more interested in building a relationship with who I thought would be my intended. (smile) I finally applied and was accepted.

I waited, while as an exchange student overseas, looking forward to the day that I would return, and what could happen in my relationship with this guy. About a month before my return, he called, and we had a long and pleasant conversation. It was an expensive call. I was so grateful and thrilled that I sent one of my photos expressing my gratitude. Upon returning to Jamaica, I thought it strange that he did not call. I waited and when I called, he sounded so neutral. I was troubled. Nothing was said to me about this new relationship that he was pursuing with a mutual friend, with whom I had spoken to about my interest in this person. How I found out took the breath out of me.

I was traveling in a car with one of my church elders who, not knowing of my "connection" to this guy, began talking about him and our mutual friend being in a relationship, and some spinoffs from that association. The elder's wife knew, as I had shared with her, and she began to reach her hand behind towards me in the backseat. I was startled. I did not want anyone to touch me. I was hurt by the news. I felt so many conflicting emotions all at once. I thought he and I had a real-ationship. How could he have hidden this from me, and for me to find out this way? I was writing a play at the time for my drama group to put on for the public. For two weeks, even with much encouragement from my drama director (thank you Dawn), my creative juices dried up. She waited patiently, but as the time was running out, she had to challenge me to rise up and I did.

It turned out that he chose to marry this friend. I was devastated, especially because I had convinced myself that he was the person to whom God was referring, and I had opened my heart (left it unguarded). I was invited to the wedding and I went, not knowing how I would survive this one. God was so good to me that someone who was going to perform in the wedding, had taken her baby and asked me if I could keep the child for her. It was my pleasure. I realized later that this was like "divine distraction". This child was a pleasure to have at our table. The pain intensified that night as my imagination would not settle down. The thought of him being with someone else in the place where I thought I should have been. I accepted this marriage mentally, but I still had a heart struggle for a few years. Another how come question, especially where God was concerned. I fought to get this now married man out of my system. I ended up in a rebound relationship with another fine young man, but because I was still battling and dealing with my heart concerning the first one, I could not settle down immediately. I found myself after a while comparing the two men. The latter relationship could not have survived. We had to end it for that and other reasons.

I battled with God. I battled with my own emotions. I battled with the "talks" around me. It was not a secret that I was attracted to my friend who was now married. We were a part of the same group. Young people are not always kind to each other. I heard the comments being made and some were embarrassing. I am taking the time and space to relate this encounter so that you my readers, if you have or are experiencing anything similar, will know that the world does not end because we are brokenhearted. Life does not stop because we have lost what we thought to be the best thing we have ever had. It may take a while, but this too will pass.

Eventually, the day came that I was freed (Hallelujah!) I rejoiced. Too much of my youthful emotional energy was spent battling this situation. I had to destroy anything that I had – notes, writings, pictures, etc. that could have connected my emotions to him – soul ties. What really was the turning point had to do with my real-ationship with God. As I battled with this awful twist in my "love drama" and wondering how God could do this to me. I came upon a verse in the Bible that shot through me like an arrow, and brought the deepest conviction within. "..let God be true, but every man a liar..." (Romans 3:4 – KJV) I realized then that God is never a liar. He is not a deceiver. He does not play games with us. If something does not work out the way we expected it to, we always have to judge ourselves and not God! He makes no mistakes. When that simple truth profoundly hit me that day, I humbled my heart and confessed to Him. I said: "You are always true O God; I am the liar." It truly was a humbling moment for me. We should have no place in our hearts to accuse God of wrongdoing, though it is tempting for us to do so when we are confused about our circumstances, and how He works in them.

I saw my "married friend" after two plus decades of not seeing him. He was open and friendly but felt like a stranger to me. This surprised me to the point where I had to ask myself if there was any unforgiveness still left in my heart towards him. I felt closer to

246

his wife than to him. I knew I had forgiven them, but what a transformation compared to what I had felt for him decades before! You see, I was no longer believing that he was the promised one for me. I had worked through all of that. I realized that the only thing that linked me in such a horrible soul tie was my mind – what I believed should have been. When I let it go...it let me go! I could relate freely but not feeling any connection to him at all. The feeling I had after seeing him again was, if we were both single at this time, and he was in a line of men to choose from, I don't know that I would choose him. Did I eventually find such a person to whom I felt God was referring? Yes. My current husband fits the bill. After trials and failures with a couple males, I am glad that I did not give up hope in God. I am happy that I continued to trust Him with all the blunders I have made. This is where rubber hits the road; when it comes to matters of the heart in our real-ationship with God.

Abusive Relationship

The second major trauma that tested my "faithfulness regardless" could have wiped me out spiritually came when I was attacked, this time, not by a stranger; and I was now an adult and in full-time ministry – an intercessor. The worst incident was when I was slammed into a wall and when I screamed for help, I was thrown on a couch and a cushion was pressed into my face while I was held down! Rape was not the motive, but control. I was suffocating and not strong enough to get my assailant off. It seemed like eternity and I was in shock. When the person released me, I sat up just staring. I felt like I was about to lose my mind! For the first time in all my Christian life (18 yrs. serving the Lord), I blocked God completely from my mind! Weird, I know, but this was the only way I could keep my sanity. I could not believe that serving the Lord as I did, He could have allowed this to be happening to me. I could not wrap my mind around it so the safest thing to do, in the moment, was to not even think – and especially about where my Father was when all this was happening. Again, I had to go through a healing process, but it was difficult to speak about this. There were some Christian songs I could not sing during that period, but I kept on praying, not just for myself but for others who were experiencing similar struggles. That came from my training in intercession. For me, it was "Lord help me!" prayers. I felt like a cripple – spiritually. It took me about 5 years to truly recover from the trauma. That period of my life was spent trying to understand God and working out the "How come?" part of it. For about one year, I did not do any public speaking. I had to get some answers.

I knew I could not give up on God, but I needed those answers. Slowly they came. "God is a good God and He can never be otherwise." "Bad things do happen to good people and good things happen to bad people." I learnt that as long as we live on this side of eternity, there is evil present in the world which can touch anyone of us, the Christian included. In spite of my blocking my Heavenly Father, He stood close to me and He comforted me. He kept speaking to me even through formations in the sky. He was gentle and patient with me, and my faith began to rise again.

I wanted to serve Him again with my WHOLE HEART, and for the strong faith and trust that I had in Him from a child, to return. He and I had walked through too many things before. There were too many occasions of His goodness and grace in my life for me to let Him go, but it hurt real bad that my Heavenly Dad permitted someone to attack me like that. One thing that also helped me was the fact that my Heavenly Father did not spare His own Son (Jesus) suffering on the cross, and He loved Him – this was His Beloved Son. I was comforted by this. A few years later when I confronted my attacker, I was told by him that his intention was not to kill me but to muzzle me. I had to forgive again and press on. I do want to challenge here, any male or female who attacks another person physically, to consider if the shoe were on the other foot, how you would interpret such an attack. Simply as a joke? A simple exercise to send a message?

A third test came when I just could not get pregnant with the biological clock running out. I have always heard, "It is God who opens the womb; why wasn't He opening mine? I would be raising my child/ren to love Him. What's up God? It finally happened. My husband and I were elated. We even started making some lifestyle changes. Then came the miscarriage. The memories of the many discarded pregnancy test kits, the painful examinations;

the struggle with endometriosis that seem to have been blocking my chances, all flooded my mind. For those of you who have experienced this –hearing those pieces plop into the toilet bowl involuntarily, while you helplessly listen, and have to let that child go is not nice. Giving my husband the news I knew he did not want to hear – "Honey, we lost the battle". Not nice. This was after seeing the glee on his face only months before when the doctor confirmed that I was pregnant. I was devastated. We were heart-broken. I had always wanted 3 children – now I might not have any?! My option left was adoption and it was not an afterthought. We had always planned that at least one of our 3 would be an adopted child that we would love as our own. I am glad that we went ahead. He turned 15 during the writing of this book. He was born the month when the baby I lost was due to be born. What a God!

Something happened though that reminded me of the faithfulness of God even during this painful loss. When my obstetrician saw me that fateful morning, and the bleeding had not stopped, she prayed with me. As she prayed, I remember asking God for three things: "God", I said. "If it is in Your providential will that I cannot have this child in spite of all my faith now, please do this for me: (i) Let Devon, my husband be at home; (2) Don't let anyone else be at my home and (3) Let it happen in my home. Well, it happened as I requested. A nurse was visiting and had just left when I went to the bathroom. Then it happened. Amidst my grief, I was thankful that He answered that request.

I still grappled with, why do great couples not conceive or if they do, only to lose it? I didn't know the answer. Why do those jumping out of trees, drinking all kinds of potions and doing all the wrong things while pregnant still have the baby? I don't know. It was one of those mysteries that I had to embrace and move on – being faithful to Jesus, regardless. Remembering what my good High School and present-day friend Shar had told me while I was going through various crisis experiences: (a) "Don't ever let the devil accuse God to you." (b) "God might not change the winter but He will provide a winter coat"; and (c), "God is a Redeemer". My good friends and my Christian brethren were the winter coats at times. Not sure how I would have made it through without them.

Another major test of my wholeheartedness to God came in 2006 when I was getting ready to go to preach at my church. Title of the message: "When God Does Not Make Sense" based on the book of Job. While dressing, my husband ran upstairs with an anxious look in his eyes, enquiring if I had seen our 3+ yr. old son (who we had from 5 months old, had gotten legal guardianship for and loved very much). I went downstairs to help them look. Nightfall came. No sight of him. The police, fire brigade and cesspool people all filled the parking lot. He was later pulled from a manhole that was left uncovered in the play area of the apartment where we were living. The cesspool persons had come and done a job 2 days before. Several persons could have been culpable.

While waiting for them to pull the pit to check, I left the crowd and went back upstairs praying. When I heard the scream from the crowd, I knew they found him. I couldn't pray but I remember thinking, "Let him be alive Lord" although hours had passed and, "Don't let the crowd rush up here." The latter was a simple prayer, but it was heard. Only 2 significant persons came to give me the news I did not want to hear. It was Shar and a neighbour. At the hospital he was pronounced dead. Another shock! I immediately thought of his biological parents, his mother pregnant and soon to deliver! Apart from our own trauma, how were we going to break this news to them, which had to happen soon? I was numb and feeling faint!

When I reached home from the hospital with friends and family in our apartment, I was between fainting and dying. I didn't know which one. A voice whispered, "Take out your sermon notes and read what you wrote." I had written, "The Lord gives, and the Lord takes away, Blessed be the name of the Lord". I had written that Job's response to his tragedies, losing all of his children in one blow was to worship. I had written that cursing God and encouraging others to do the same (Job's wife's response) was never the right choice when facing difficulties and tragedies. Beloved...now it was my turn! Could I move forward? How was I going to move forward? How was I going to explain to others how such a tragedy befell two Ministers of Religion? It was not easy.

We slept on the living room floor for several nights. Our appetite went, although people kept bringing food. Any interest in pleasure was gone! Telling his parents was one of the hardest things we have ever done. Yet, God was there with us and for us. The brethren swamped us with calls, cards, visits, hundreds of messages on our three phones that we could not clear. Funeral expenses were paid without us asking for a cent. What we had sown in praying for others we were now receiving back with interest! What a God!

So here I stand today, made strong by the Almighty. Since all of this I have been able to write two books and am finishing off this one. I have experienced a Real God who gave me Real Grace to go through some harsh realities in a Real World of the good, the bad and the indifferent.

I Have Learnt:
- o To be faithful to God and wholeheartedly serve and worship Him regardless (Philippians 4:11-13)

- o Unless the Lord builds my house (life) I would be a miserable failure trying to build it on my own (Psalm 127:1) o If I had hope in this world alone, forget it. (1 Corinthians 15:19)

o There are some mysteries about life and about God that we will never solve, but we trust Him anyway. His heart is always pure and good towards His people (Jeremiah 29:11)

o About the Proverbs 31 ideal woman in the Bible, that "her lamp goes not out, but it burns continually through the night [of trouble, privation, or sorrow, warning away fear, doubt and mistrust].

o That God can help us to have a Prepared Response that can help us through any given situation. Knowing the Bible prepares us for what our righteous response should be in given situations (2 Timothy 4:2)

o That understanding the Purpose (if not specific but even in principle) for our pain, propels us in a hopeful future, trusting God because His intent is for our scars to one day become our stars; someone else will make it through a dark night because of how we shine for God through our trials (2 Corinthians 1:3-5)

o Everyone has a story. Your story, if you wholeheartedly continue to serve God, will work out for your good, and you will be a blessing to many. (Romans 8:28)

You may be reading this chapter as a broken person, believing that God has cast you aside, or is unresponsive to your cry. The truth is, even when we sin, and Israel did so many times, when they cried to God, He heard and came and delivered them.

What To Do If You Have Failed God

a) Humbly go to Him and simply ask for His forgiveness

b) Request that He comes into your heart and life and help you to do what He wills you to do with your life

c) Ask Him for the grace to live every day for Him as He builds His character in you

d) Know that He will never leave you nor forsake you

e) Go every day to Him with confidence in prayer, reading His love letter to you (the Holy Bible)

f) Let Him lead you to a Bible-believing Church where you can have fellowship with others as you find your purpose, giftings and calling in Him.

This I have done since I was fifteen years old and He has never failed me yet. He will not fail you. I have lived my life serving the Lord Jesus Christ, having the hope that I will spend eternity with Him when He returns for His own. Another hope and confidence I have is that I will see my two children who have gone ahead of me. What a great day of reunion that will be when we get to heaven. Please ensure that you deal with a broken relationship or the absence of a real-ationship with God so you can live with Him eternally. What a hope! I love Him so much, don't you?

As I have been writing this book – true to form and just as God indicated to me, it was not an easy task. As dynamic and as roller-coaster as aspects of our real-ationships are, so was the writing of this book. This was about real-writing. Reality checks while writing. It was a great journey however. Some of my real-ationships have been deepened. Some new ones have been formed and have changed my life forever. How can one live without real-ationships? No amount of social media contacts can replace our face-to-face, rubbing shoulders, working and relating side-by-side real-ationships.

Trusting that now that you have read, even if only portions of this book, you will be changed forever – gaining a deep appreciation of who you have that's contributing to your growth in real-ationships. Trusting that in dealing with your enemies, you will grow too from the painful experiences you have had with them. Trusting that you now have that real-ationship with God that no one can take from you, and He will not allow you to be snatched from His Hand.

Stay tuned for the next in this series – looking at real-ationships in the workplace; in ministry; in business, etc. that can make us or break us.

BIBLIOGRAPHY

1. Harbajan, Maria. ARISE…Intercessors Arise! A Manual for the Birthing, Calling, Training and Restoration of Prayer Warriors, Outskirts Press, Colorado, USA, 2015:

2. Article on "Grieving the Loss of a Child". American Association For Marriage And Family Therapy. [https://www.aamft.org/imis15/AAMFT/Content/Consumer_Updates/Grieving_the_Loss_of_A_Child.aspx

   [http://www1.cbn.com/700club/do-yourself-favorforgive-interview-joyce-meyer]

3. Article: The Gleaner, Sun. April 24, 2016 [http://ww.jamaica-gleaner.com/article/lead-stories/20160424/secret-gardens-all-cried-out-monument-remember-children-killed-across}

4. Adapted from *The Five Love Languages Singles Edition* by Dr. Gary Chapman. www.fivelovelanguages.com.

5. https://www.psychologytoday.com/us/blog/the-urban-scientist/201003/how-spot-friends-enemies-frenemies-and-bullies

ABOUT THE AUTHOR

Maria L. Harbajan is President and CEO of the National Intercessory Prayer Network of Jamaica and Prayer Centre of the Caribbean (NIPNOJ/PCOC). She is an ordained minister and has been involved in the ministry of intercession for over 30 years. She is host of a radio programme, *"ARISE AND BUILD JAMAICA"*, which is aired on LOVE FM in Jamaica.

Mrs. Harbajan has known Jesus as her personal Saviour since she was 15 years old. She attended Jamaica Theological Seminary graduating with a Bachelor's Degree in Theology; and went on to obtain her Master's degree in Counselling Psychology at the Caribbean Graduate School of Theology. She also holds a Doctorate in Ministry, from Central Christian University and did Leadership studies at the Haggai Institute in Singapore in 2000. Mrs. Harbajan entered full-time ministry for two years ('85 - '87), paused to study and resumed in 1991.

She is a member of the International Prayer Council as convener of the Caribbean Prayer Summit which has been held in Barbados, Suriname and Jamaica. She is also founder of, and senior counsellor at the OASIS Counselling Services and OASIS

Restoration Ministries International, a ministry that seeks to restore individuals, families, businesses, etc. to their purpose in God. A speaker at conferences, camps, schools, churches, etc., she covers a variety of topics including Family and Marital Relationships, Intercession, Spiritual Warfare, Stress Management, Issues Involving Young People, and personal issues that affect people in the workplace. She has ministered internationally in the Middle East, Africa, Asia, Europe, North, Central and South America.

Mrs. Harbajan is involved in Missions, teaching pastors and other leaders on the Mission field. A leader at the Portmore Gospel Assembly, St. Catherine, Jamaica, she is married to Devon Harbajan, a Minister of Religion and they have a son DeMario Samuel, and daughter-mentee – Jenene, as well as many spiritual children.

For further information: **MARIA HARBAJAN, DMin, M.A., B.Th.**
President and CEO, National Intercessory Prayer Network of Jamaica
Founder/Senior Counsellor, OASIS Counselling Services
Founder, OASIS Restoration Ministries International
Regional Coordinator, Caribbean Prayer Summit
Member of the Executive, International Prayer Council
Call 876-806-4921(m) or 876-967-4041 (office)
E-mail address: mardevharb@gmail.com